SWIMMING LONDON

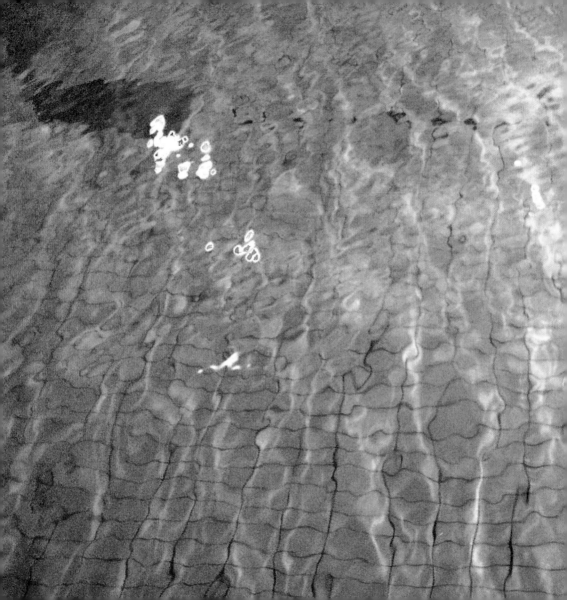

SWIMMING LONDON

THE 50 BEST POOLS, LIDOS, LAKES AND RIVERS FROM AROUND THE CAPITAL

JENNY LANDRETH

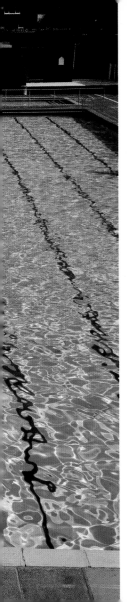

CONTENTS

SWIMMING LONDON

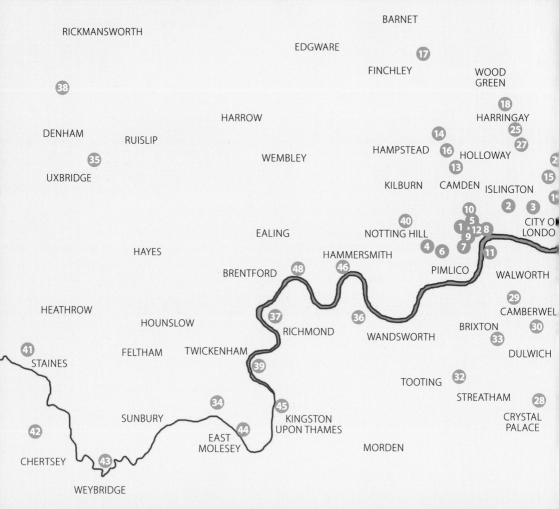

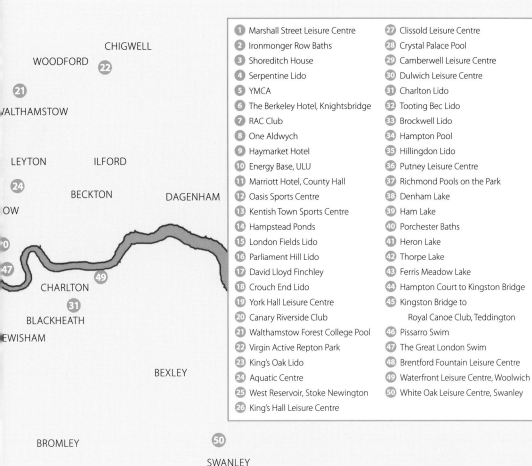

LOUGHTON

CHIGWELL

WOODFORD

WALTHAMSTOW

LEYTON   ILFORD

BECKTON   DAGENHAM

OW

CHARLTON

BLACKHEATH

LEWISHAM

BEXLEY

BROMLEY

SWANLEY

1 Marshall Street Leisure Centre
2 Ironmonger Row Baths
3 Shoreditch House
4 Serpentine Lido
5 YMCA
6 The Berkeley Hotel, Knightsbridge
7 RAC Club
8 One Aldwych
9 Haymarket Hotel
10 Energy Base, ULU
11 Marriott Hotel, County Hall
12 Oasis Sports Centre
13 Kentish Town Sports Centre
14 Hampstead Ponds
15 London Fields Lido
16 Parliament Hill Lido
17 David Lloyd Finchley
18 Crouch End Lido
19 York Hall Leisure Centre
20 Canary Riverside Club
21 Walthamstow Forest College Pool
22 Virgin Active Repton Park
23 King's Oak Lido
24 Aquatic Centre
25 West Reservoir, Stoke Newington
26 King's Hall Leisure Centre

27 Clissold Leisure Centre
28 Crystal Palace Pool
29 Camberwell Leisure Centre
30 Dulwich Leisure Centre
31 Charlton Lido
32 Tooting Bec Lido
33 Brockwell Lido
34 Hampton Pool
35 Hillingdon Lido
36 Putney Leisure Centre
37 Richmond Pools on the Park
38 Denham Lake
39 Ham Lake
40 Porchester Baths
41 Heron Lake
42 Thorpe Lake
43 Ferris Meadow Lake
44 Hampton Court to Kingston Bridge
45 Kingston Bridge to
      Royal Canoe Club, Teddington
46 Pissarro Swim
47 The Great London Swim
48 Brentford Fountain Leisure Centre
49 Waterfront Leisure Centre, Woolwich
50 White Oak Leisure Centre, Swanley

INTRODUCTION

I was sitting in the sauna at Tooting Lido, warming up after a winter swim when conversation got round to what we were up to. 'I'm writing a book on the best places to swim in London,' I volunteered. 'That'll be a short book,' said a fellow swimmer. He told me about the thousands of great pools in every town in Germany, where he came from. I was impressed. 'There are more 50-metre pools in Paris than in the whole of the UK,' said another swimmer, confidently. Lucky Parisians, I thought. We started to talk about London's now-defunct pools and lidos, about how 'progress' sometimes doesn't feel like progress at all. And I worked out that sharing the remaining dozen or so public outdoor pools between more than 8 million London residents means we really do all have to squeeze up and take turns. I came out of the sauna hot and bothered: why can't we be more like Germany, or Paris? The capital definitely needs more lidos and more Olympic size pools.

But I've realised, in writing this book, that what we do have, what we do very well, is diversity. Hot, cold, indoor, outdoor, natural, posh, definitely-not-posh, exclusive, inclusive, fun, serious, long, short, historic, architectural, falling down, glamorous, high, low, huge and tiny. It should come as no surprise since we are a diverse city, and one that is built around water. We even divide ourselves according to which side of the river we live on (only half jokingly). So for diversity, which features in this book in all its glory, London is a fantastic city to swim in.

To create this 'best of', I swam in as many pools as I could that I thought reflected the diversity of what the city has to offer. But ultimately, omissions and preferences are mine, and some of them may not reflect your own tastes. I have a secret penchant for pools that are kindly described as down at heel, which might deter the more fastidious swimmer. And I'm a hardy outdoor unheated type; I can be found jumping into water where lifeguards have kindly broken the ice, an addiction that remains niche. But if one pool is not your cup of tea, I can guarantee that there will be some in here that absolutely are, because this is a collection of the best London has to offer – from free to very pricey, and from huge old beasts to trim modern tanks.

For the purposes of this book, I defined 'London' as 'within the M25'. I'm sad to report that there were a few pools I couldn't get into, usually by dint of protective membership secretaries who didn't share my fondness for bending the rules. Pools that I would dearly have loved to include. But my rule of thumb was that if I could get into them, then so could a casual reader. And if I really couldn't, however hard I pleaded, then chances were, you wouldn't be able to, either. There seemed no point in celebrating the uber-exclusive for the sake of it.

Swimming makes me happy. It's a key part of my life. I feel better when I do it, and I've never (yet) regretted a swim. So be you fast or slow, skilled or happy amateur, wetsuited or no – I wish you happy swimming, and much of it.

Jenny Landreth

MARSHALL STREET LEISURE CENTRE

The history of this tiny part of London is fascinating, though not always conducive to a relaxing swim. In the mid-1600s the area was named, with admirably blunt logic, Pesthouse Close because it was where plague victims lived together in isolation as an alternative to being barricaded into their homes, with resident doctors attempting to alleviate their suffering. It may sound charitable but the aim was also to prevent the spread of the disease; a burial ground, known as a plague pit, was also on site, to relieve the pressure on local churchyards.

In what way would this history unsettle your swim? It shouldn't – if you can stop your imagination from wandering downwards, deep underground. Simply don't think about the fact that resting beneath the marble base of the pool, right under your vigorously splashing feet, lies an ancient burial ground for thousands of plague victims who died in agony.

This pool certainly does 'atmosphere' brilliantly. It's a glorious hushed space that evokes reverence and purpose in a swimmer; everything is tasteful and elegant. There's a classic white and blue domed ceiling, and a contemporary frosty blue-green on the walls. There's a beautifully appointed and gently lit balustrade. At one end is a bronze sculpture of a merbaby riding two dolphins. And the pool itself is a great cool slab of marble, with a scoop taken out at one end to give us depth. The marble is no longer pristine, it's marked and cracked in places, but that serves to add more of a sense of Grade II listed history. There's only one visual jar: the alarmingly red oversized and over-frequent depth signs that spoil the sweep of one wall.

Marshall Street Leisure Centre is a historic pool fantastically brought into the 21st century.

The first 'Baths' were built on what became Marshall Street in 1851; then in 1928 a new building was erected, with a first-class swimming 'bath' measuring 100 feet by 35 feet. This included a smaller second-class bath, slipper baths (which are actual household baths as we might know them, supposedly shaped like slippers), a public laundry, and a maternity and child welfare centre. That first-class 'bath' is the one that stands today, and there's an old brass plaque on the entrance door saying 'maternity centre' to remind you of the heritage. The whole place has been subject to recent renovation, though the pool is clearly the star attraction. The changing rooms are more

The merboy is just one of the carefully maintained details at the shallow end of the 100 ft pool.

of a changing corridor, with generous locker space but less generous room to manoeuvre, but this is a small price to pay – which is more than you can say for the entrance fee. Still, this is central London, and this is our star public pool, and one of my favourites.

Marshall Street Leisure Centre

Address 15 Marshall Street, Soho, London W1F 7EL
Phone 0207 871 7222
Web www.better.org.uk/leisure/marshall-street -leisure-centre

IRONMONGER ROW BATHS

There's so much history attached to this building it's impossible to do it justice in this confined space. It seems particularly apt, then, that the building works on this latest incarnation were delayed by months because of archaeological finds on site. It's Grade II listed and dates from 1931, and the full story is on the walls of the building itself, decorated as they are with storyboards detailing how the pool moved from the old days into the new. The oral histories from locals, stories of parents watching galas, of newly arrived immigrants finding a sense of home, of a community gathered round water, are quite some testament to the power inherent in a building.

A massive cream stone slab above the entrance into which the words 'Ironmonger Row Baths' are carved seems highly symbolic of this power. It's modern but permanent and substantial; it is craftsmanship. A simple black and white sign strapped to the side of the building, with the word 'BATHS' running down it, replaces one that mysteriously used to say 'Swimming. Turkish Baths. Contours.' That they kept the original name, too, rather than Leisure-Centrifying it, is indicative of how seriously the building's past has been taken and what it represents. This balancing act of old and new is a tricky one to pull off – have they done it?

Inside, this celebrated pool has been lovingly brought into a new era. You get a first glimpse through a letterbox window in reception (and thus, obviously, a view of reception while you swim). It is set in a stylish hall

From this viewpoint you can clearly see how the pool slides into the deep end.

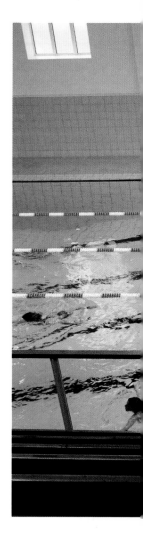

with great detailing – the spectator seats, for instance, look more like church pews – and there's little of that garish plastic that pervades most pools; the colour scheme is a delicate beige, white and Hail Mary blue, heritage over fashion. There's lots of natural light through sizeable windows including a flat, glazed ice-cream wafer right down the centre of the ceiling, which is a harmonious shallow curve. The pool itself is 33m long, sloping down in gentle ledges until it drops into a proper deep end. That it is an infinity pool detailed with pristine white tiles gives a clean simplicity to the whole atmosphere, which is very attractive, very calm. There's a separate children's pool but it's a shame that they didn't return the diving boards to the deep end.

There is much to admire in the rest of the building, too. A cool modern marble staircase leads to the gallery, which includes a carefully restored original slipper bath with working tap. You can then walk down an original staircase, to a hallway from the old building, and into a modern community laundry. You'll find more of the story told on boards in little side annexes. Downstairs, they've treated the famous Turkish Hammam with the same respect; you can get modern spa treatments there but it's hard to beat the beautifully refurbished traditional hot and cold rooms.

It is worth spending some time wandering around the building enjoying the restored features, including the staircase above.

Ironmonger Row Baths

Address Ironmonger Row, 1 Norman Street, London EC1V 3AA
Phone 0203 642 5520
Web www.better.org.uk/leisure/ironmonger-row-baths

SHOREDITCH HOUSE

Shoreditch House is tucked away on a quiet side street called Ebor Street and is the younger sister of the more famous, and first in the 'House' family, Soho House. It's a private club and has the understated air of 'exclusive' about it – not in a gold chandelier way, but in a discreet, keep your voice down way. As required in Shoreditch, it's cutting-edge stylish. There's a lot of stainless steel (more of which later), walls rough-lined in distressed wood planks, and the requisite mix of trendily upcycled and new furniture.

The pool is on the roof – a combination of words that always holds the promise of great things, of a particular kind of louche glamour, of views at least. To get there visitors need to take a small shiny lift up to the changing facilities, where you can grab towels and robes. On the reception sits a small wood-edged blackboard of the kind children used in schools in the 1950s on which is written, in coloured chalk, 'Pool temp: 28°'. That's warm. If the changing space is smallish, the showers are positively chunky. There are black floors, white brick-shaped tiles and copious amounts of free product.

Then it's through a big industrial door outside and up some hammered metal stairs – they have really worked the 'adapted factory' raw-material feel – and finally onto the roof, which does indeed have the louche glamour it promised. The walkway is narrow at the sides with one entire glass wall looking inside, but there is more space at either end, leaving room for great fat recliners. Beyond the pool there's another area crammed with comfy loungers and day beds, so-called because a day could easily be whiled away on them. But what really makes it worth coming up here is the tremendous view. Through a protective metal mesh, you've got

High-tech meets low-tech meets upcycle in London's best posing pool.

enough height to see right over the big shiny workings of the City; it's a dynamic visual treat, mostly square blocks and soaring glass slithers, a cuboid skyline broken only by the fat bullet end of the Gherkin.

The pool itself is small, and here's more stainless steel, the lining. It's infinity edged, and the same depth throughout, which should make for a fast swim, but serious swimming is not the gig here. The length is only 20m, for a start. Then there's the fact that you feel like a tiny person swimming in a giant's sink. It's definitely a place for posing rather than snapping on a rubber hat. Swimming head-up lets you really make the most of that view, the real reason to be here. Then a post-swim sauna and you can head back out into Shoreditch looking definitely, defiantly, cool.

The only roof-top pool in London gives a fantastic view of the City.

Shoreditch House

Address
Ebor Street, Shoreditch,
London E1 6AW
Phone
0207 739 5040
Web
www.shoreditchhouse.com

SERPENTINE LIDO

If you are the kind of person who gets a small thrill at the almost anarchic thought of being nearly naked in a Royal Park, this is the lido for you. If you are the kind of person averse to swimming in goose poo, even from royal geese, it is not.

This lido is very well documented both from a historical perspective (the lake it is part of was commissioned by Queen Caroline in 1730) and a sporting one (the 10K open-water Olympic races were swum here in 2012); and barely a winter goes past without newspaper coverage of the Christmas morning swims here, which may involve breaking ice and definitely requires a certain mindset. It's the only natural outdoor swim in central London, open early every morning of the year to members of the Serpentine Swimming Club, and to the public from June to early September. The water is cleaner now than it ever has been. Originally fed from the River Westbourne, it now comes from three boreholes, one of which is beside the nearby Princess Diana Memorial Fountain, itself a great diversion if swimming in the lido is not diversion enough.

Once you've paid and used the tiny changing room, there's a landscaped area with a café, a very small baby pool where smart London nannies hang out, and a neat lawn available for sprawling on. The entrance to the lido is across a small bridge over a public path and down the steps the other side. For first-time visitors, it is only when you are halfway across the bridge in your

The Serpentine is home to tourists in pedalos and swimmers alike.

costume that you start to appreciate how odd this might look to people on the path below. It's an opportunity to unleash one's inner show-off maybe, using that tiny bridge as a stage and dancing across, as if the people passing underneath were a willing audience.

The swimming area of the lake is marked clearly by a string of white sausage buoys. A small jetty with a ladder pokes out across the width at one end or there's an easy slope with railings at the side. On a warm day, stepping off the path and committing to the water feels easy, until you watch your feet disappear under thick ochre liquid. My best advice is not to look down as your toes squish into the settled gunk. Once in, the water feels soft, textured almost, but visibility is poor. You can thrash up and down the line of buoys but all you'll see with your head down is a green-yellow-brown, like swimming through melted tweed. This is what it is to swim in a lake. They are living, unpredictable and wholly natural. For the converted, to have access to nature slap-bang in the middle of a massive urban space is fabulous.

You may find yourself sharing your swim with some ducks, but there's a cold shower on the pavement to wash off all the gunk. And there's a bench on which to rest and reflect on what you've just done. Whether you swam a mile or ten metres, that's a rare kind of bliss.

There are fewer greater solitary experiences than having the Serpentine to yourself.

Serpentine Lido

Address
Hyde Park, London
W2 3XA
Phone
0207 706 3422
Web
www.royalparks.org.uk

YMCA

YMCA is a members' health, social and fitness club, just off Tottenham Court Road, right in the heart of 'cheap electronics stores' London. The YMCA has existed here for over a hundred years and there's a remnant, a now anomalous-looking grandfather clock and ancient portrait, in what otherwise looks like the smart entrance to an underground car park.

Inside is like being in a huge secret bunker. There's so much London up top, you can easily forget that there's a lot going on down under our crammed pavements too. After the narrow bottleneck of the reception area, you go down some stairs and an underground world opens in front of you: cafés, gyms, indoor courts and people scurrying round in sportswear. And of course, the pool, which you get your first glimpse of through the café window. It's hard to work out whether the spaces were carved from great concrete blocks or are delineated by them; the décor is definitely a mix of engine-fumed brutal and student lounge.

The changing rooms are also a mix, treading the line between corporate and public, private and social. Not as flash as top-end, not grotty low-rent, stylish showers balanced by more prosaic white-painted brick walls. It's had a good revamp, they are clean and spacious with plenty of lockers and small bench areas. Having changed, you go – and this feels a bit odd – up two flights of a spiral staircase to the pool. I say 'odd' because two flights is long enough to make you believe you've gone the wrong way, worry that any second now a door will open and you'll be turfed out, in your swimming costume, onto Tottenham Court Road.

The 25m pool is lined with dark-blue and black tiles, not a colour scheme

What lies beneath the surface of London's streets is sometimes just as impressive as what's above.

associated with swimming, but it works here because it is a reminder that you're underground. Even the underwater lighting is dim and blue. This is the pool for the subterranean or nocturnal among us. It has a quiet aura, dark and intent. It's a busy, well-used pool, but there are little oases of calm in the day. Swimming is essentially a solitary activity, and the design of this place emphasises that: you're surrounded by cafés and activity on the other side of the glass wall, but cocooned from the busy noise of it. In one of the most crammed parts of the city, the pool offers refuge.

What else makes this pool stand out? Run by a charity, it has a mixed clientele. Yes, there are the students and visitors you'd expect of a YMCA, along with corporate membership and a strong community element.

Not simply a great swimming experience, the YMCA deserves special mention for the work it does with HIV swimmers.

But the most inspiring thing they do is their 'Positive Health' programme. Since 1997 the pool has been running a swimming group for people living with HIV; it's the first of its kind, run by dedicated staff who understand the issues an HIV-positive person might face. HIV can leave people with compromised health, which can be improved by managing fitness. But the group also offers valuable contact time and a social element. Levels go from beginners up to pre-club, and it's been such a great success that people from the group now have swim-coach qualifications. You get a sense that the staff have real pride in this, and in their centre as a whole – and that feels right. The ASA agree: in 2011 Positive Health won the award for 'Community Project of the Year'.

YMCA Club

Address
112 Great Russell Street,
London WC1B 3NQ
Phone
0207 343 1700
Web
www.ymcaclub.co.uk

THE BERKELEY HOTEL, KNIGHTSBRIDGE

Sometimes one's ideas of what constitutes a good swim can be challenged in the most surprising of locations. Knightsbridge, particularly five-star hotels therein, are not my natural home. But it was in the five-star Berkeley Hotel (where non-residents can join the Health Spa) on the edge of Hyde Park where I started off with one opinion and ended with another. This is one of the glories of water.

On the seventh floor of this building you'd expect great views, and you get them. To one side, you see over the southern edge of Hyde Park, all gravel drives and perfectly manicured planting; to the other, the less-ordered roofs of Knightsbridge catch your eye.

The pool itself seems to have been imagined around a Roman bath: it's a deep, dark box of water, historic in look, surrounded by stone pillars and with a stone edge. The depth markings are engraved into the stone, and there is plenty of marble and tiny mosaic tiles, as you might expect in this part of London. The ceiling is shabbier, a large wooden flaky-painted panel. The sloping steps on either side take up most of one end, but still, it only takes me seven front-crawl arms to get across or five breaststrokes. So, it's small. And hot. And yes, very glamorous with the loungers around and the juices and glossy magazines as well as access to a small terrace lined with box hedge and camellia all the way up here on the seventh floor.

The fact that I'd counted strokes and they were few shows not just the size of the pool, but my mood. This is not swimming, I was muttering to myself, this is hot wading. And then another woman got in. Head up, hat- and goggle-free, she slowly and purposefully glided from one end of the

When the panelled roof is open on a sunny day, the pool reveals its true glory.

pool to the other. I flipped and spun like a mad puppy, trying to get rid of my excess vigour, and she happily pushed herself across, one calm and peaceful length after another. Eventually, we were at one end at the same time, and smiled at each other. 'Isn't this utter bliss?' she said. 'When they open the roof in the summer, there is nowhere I'd rather be.' I looked at the tired wooden ceiling, and thought – it opens! And then suddenly I got it. I thought about that extra view, the most unexpected one, that delicious bonus square of blue, and I knew that would feel fantastic.

'I understand,' I said. 'I love swimming under the sky.' Some days it's thrash thrash thrash. And some days, swimming can be about pottering up and down, stretching out, just feeling your limbs moving gently in ways they otherwise wouldn't. This is the kind of pool for that. Slow down, relax, and enjoy the sky.

The Berkeley

Address Wilton Place, Knightsbridge, London SW1X 7RL
Phone 0207 201 1699
Web www.the-berkeley.co.uk

This is about as far from
Tooting Bec Lido as you
can get.

RAC CLUB

Be in no doubt: this is right at the centre of a very particular kind of privilege. Establishment, old-boy privilege, royal privilege even, since (if one listens to whispers) the Queen was taught to swim here. The dates do fit at a pinch – she was born in 1926, and there was no pool at Buckingham Palace until 1938, so this could have been her London pool until she was 12. She would only have got in, of course, on a 'daughters or wives' ticket – now, it's progressed a little, and women can be members, as long as they are dressed with 'commensurate formality', which fortunately means a standard swimming costume.

The location is Pall Mall, and the building is all railings and carriage lamps and huge revolving doors; at the time of writing, there was an actual car displayed in the foyer. The health club is downstairs, and on the way down the impressive carved stone staircase, you get a first glimpse of the pool. As befits one of only three Grade II listed pools in London, it looks rather special.

To call the facilities 'changing rooms' is to do them a great disservice. Through heavy wooden doors into a hushed area lit by table lamps, you are assigned a rough-curtained booth, each containing a small, dark-wood bed with crisp white linen. This is boarding school meets gentlemen's club, but not intimidatingly so – the décor is almost shabby in places. Visitors then pad past the Turkish baths, steam room, sauna and freezing plunge pool.

It looked special from the staircase, and it is. Firstly, the room is gorgeous; huge, beautifully mosaiced pillars, curved alcoves with long latticed

If you can spare the time, it's worth spending the entire day here.

windows, narrow gilt railings. It's lit by white flame lamps on narrow metal stands, and has the faded glamour of an old film star. Equally, a toga or two wouldn't look out of place, and nor does modern wicker seating. The real star, though, is the pool. It's 26.3m long and lined with Italian marble past its best, its worn beauty all adding to the charm.

The colour of the stone and the soft lighting gives the water a subtle green tinge; it's a calmer colour than that modern too-sharp blue. The water is kept at the standard 28 degrees, and it's almost a surprise to see normal lane ropes and speed signs; you'd expect something bespoke. What isn't obvious until you know it is there's no smell of chlorine: the pool has a more expensive ozone treatment, which needs comparatively tiny amounts of chlorine.

The depth change (from 1m to 2.3m) and the drop from deck to water mean this isn't a fast pool; so take it slowly and enjoy the space.

RAC Club

Address 89 Pall Mall, London SW1Y 5HS
Phone 0207 747 3365
Web www.royalautomobileclub.co.uk

Elegant and art-deco, rumour has it that the Queen learnt to swim here.

No Running

No Diving

EMERGENCY ALARM

ONE ALDWYCH HOTEL AND HAYMARKET HOTEL

There are more than a few hotels in London that offer pools, certainly too many to list here. But these two deserve a special mention since, at 17m and 18m, they are among the largest. And I'm sure you'll see why they downplay the 'swim' aspect, and highlight the 'spa'. We may know it better as 'bathing'.

One Aldwych used to be newspaper offices, and if you ignore the modern design of the atrium and focus on the huge original windows onto Aldwych (just a hefty stone's throw from the end of Fleet Street, after all) you could just about see it. An impressive feature is made of the riveted silver-painted girders that run vertically through the building. The spa/pool area is where the old printing press was – an incarnation that's about as far as it's possible to be from the original.

The pool here is small and definitely subterranean; downstairs to change, and then down more stairs to the pool. Modern art peppers the walls in bright flashes, and the pool is a 17m-long dark slab of water, like an upmarket scuba tank. Low lighting ratchets up the discreet, hushed feeling. The pool is right up against one end wall, a large

blank that's used as a film screen: on my visit, it was projecting a film of manatees blobbing gracefully through their Floridian waters – maybe chosen to make you feel better about yourself in a costume. Or maybe to underline what you'll do here – this is much more about bobbing than meaningful swimming. The constant movement of a film plays out against the dark water, and actually, though it's a consistent 1.5m throughout (nice and deep), the top of the water gets busy even with only one lazy swimmer in it.

Under the water there is another surprise: more music. It's a nice idea for this kind of place, but one that wouldn't translate into a serious swimming pool. For a start, sound changes every time your head is even partially out; and the music above and below is not coordinated, which can be jangling. Then there's the choice of music. Above the surface, it was accompanying the film, a bland, generic score. Underwater? A piece of classical music from Dvorak's New World Symphony. Lovely, you may say. But it's better known to me, an ill-educated TV addict of a certain generation, as the music from a very

particular bread advert. Such a clash of cultural inputs – five-star hotel luxury and the clogs and pushbikes of a forgotten era – set all my synapses fizzing.

The Haymarket Hotel, right off Trafalgar Square, has a pool that is also underground and a whole metre longer, at 18m. (The hotel describes it as 'vast'. That is obviously relative.) A word of warning – you have to be resident here to use the pool, so there are no changing facilities poolside. What there are poolside, in a very generous-sized space, are Chesterfield sofas in burnished white gold; the gloss of artworks bounces off the polished leather. There's also a bar. Outside holiday pools, you don't see water and alcohol in close proximity, for fairly good reasons. There are pillars, four down each side, painted in the same cold gold, with pebble mosaic round the lower part of the wall; the flooring is restored floorboards – the whole conspires to feel like it was styled after a luxe Caribbean hideaway. That's compounded with a particular effect: at one end, right across the wall, is a light display, an abstract strip of changing colours around the bright sunset spectrum. The result is a triangle of colour on water, the same triangle that occurs in nature when the sun and sea meet at the horizon. If you swim backstroke, you see the organic shapes of the soft vaulted ceiling, inset with tiny star bulbs, and for half a second you could think you were on holiday floating in the sea. There are more lights too, underwater; as you spear your front-crawl hand in, the bubbles that trail your fingers are kaleidoscopic.

The pool is elegantly mosaiced and is the same depth (1.5m) throughout. The edges are high, there's no natural catch at the end of the length. But again, despite the lane markings on the bottom, a minor addition reminds you that this place is decorative rather than useful: along one end, there's a pipe a few inches above the surface, with tiny holes, each spouting warm water; it gives a fountain effect right across. It looks beautiful. It's fun! But it gives you a moment's pause, an uncertainty, a break in your rhythm. So definitely not for serious swimming.

High glamour and comfy sofas, this is your Caribbean holiday just off Regent's Street.

One Aldwych

Address
One Aldwych, London
WC2B 4BZ
Phone
0207 300 0600
Web
www.onealdwych.com

Haymarket Hotel

Address
Haymarket Hotel,
1 Suffolk Place, London
SW1Y 4BP
Phone
0207 470 4000
Web
www.firmdalehotels.com

ENERGY BASE UNIVERSITY OF LONDON UNION (ULU)

It seems that every pool needs its Unique Selling Point (USP) and ULU is no exception. In fact, it has two. The first is 'largest pool in central London', measuring as it does 33m by 11.5m. The nearest competitor, Marshall Street, is 31m by 11m, so if you are a completist and want to be able to say, 'I've swum in the largest pool in central London,' you need to come here. It's also one of the most expensive, at £8.50 for an adult ticket, but that's a one-off day rate for the whole place and there are many student/staff concessions. Solution: plan a long swim to make it more cost-effective.

Or plan a naked one; skinny-dipping is the second, lesser-spotted USP here. For an hour every Sunday lunchtime, Naturist London organises a naked swim here, so if it's legitimate public nudity you're after, this is your place.

You might feel free once you're naked in the water, but until then you'll be reminded time and again that this is a student union; it feels

Long-since removed, ULU once hosted a Beatles photoshoot on its diving board.

Behind the facade of London's academic centre is the largest pool in central London.

like one, and the corridors smell vaguely of bacon rolls and stale nicotine. The door to the changing room looks like a janitor's cupboard, and the space beyond is not intuitive – small areas off a central corridor, toilets that are hard to find, and all done in a blue that never was and never will be fashionable, even though it's been recently made over. And if you've ever stayed in a bed and breakfast where they've shoved a shower into the corner of the bedroom, these showers will remind you of that, small plastic boxes that look terribly breakable. You get the feeling that if you pushed heavily the whole row would come down, domino-style. Still, we're not here to jump up and down on flimsy shower trays. To the pool.

This is a brute of a room that has seen better days. It was built in 1952, the Queen Mother used to watch galas here, and the Beatles did a photoshoot in 1963 with everyone larking about on the diving board (since removed), except for Ringo, who couldn't swim. There's a lot more unfashionable blue and the concrete surrounds have had their time. There are mirrors stuck randomly on the wall, and one letterbox window that looks onto the set of stairs that brought you down here.

It's a brute of a pool, too – definitely functional rather than decorative and a little too warm for my liking. But here, we're celebrating pool length, and those eight metres onto the standard 25m pool are a difference worth making. It's that extra pull, a few fewer turns and glides so you shake things up a bit, get out of your normal routine, work a bit harder. It's a visual thing too; it looks more substantial, a proper block of water, which is another reminder that it is a throwback to a long-past era. There's a proper deep end as well, and with the dropped concrete edge it all adds up to make this a slow pool. Slow, long and spacious means a good, solid workout; the word 'solid' sums up the whole thing. (Just not the showers. Don't push the showers.)

Energy Base ULU

Address Energy Base ULU, Malet Street, London WC1 7HY
Phone 0207 664 2002 **Web** www.ulu.co.uk

MARRIOTT HOTEL, COUNTY HALL

County Hall is a magnificent 1920s building in a superb location: staring defiantly across at the Houses of Parliament and Big Ben, it was the seat of the Greater London Council until that body – for which I, along with many Londoners, still have a nostalgic longing – was abolished by Margaret Thatcher. It's now most well known for hosting the London Eye on its doorstep.

The building's government history goes some way to explain the imposing interior of what is now a hotel; my great GLC memories go some way to explain how inspiring it feels to be inside it. I'd hoped – or, rather, presumed – that the pool here would be a leftover from GLC days. Why else would it be 25m? What hotel would possibly put in a pool as long as that? My presumptions were wrong: it's a new pool, installed by the hotel, in order to be distinctive. And it is: it's the largest hotel pool in London.

The light wood and wafty candles of the new spa reception area are all rather flimsy feng shui after the dark carpets and gentlemen's wingback armchairs of the hotel's council-chamber chic. Resisting the lure of a sauna or steam until after a swim, it's out the door, up the steps, through the next door, across the corridor, through another door and down some steps to the pool. Not exactly obvious, but you can't always disguise the fact that you're working within the structure of an existing building. The pool room is a huge converted attic chamber, its dimensions and the old frosted windows – one side pointing towards the river, the other side towards Waterloo – showing the heritage. And yes, a 25m pool feels distinctive in this context. The pool itself is narrow and steps intrude quite far into one side so there's really only half of it suitable for lane swimming. But it's 1.4m deep throughout and an infinity pool so people can, and do, use it for

An iconic builing in an iconic location.

A great addition to London's swimming scene, and not just for hotel guests either.

London Marriott Hotel, County Hall

Address London County Hall, Westminster Bridge Road, London SE1 7PB
Phone 0207 928 5200
Web www.marriott.co.uk

training. (You can join the gym without staying at the hotel.)

What can be slightly unnerving on a first visit is that sky right above you through a frost-filter; you're swimming high above London's busy roads, rather than in a basement as is usually the case with hotel pools, since water is so heavy. So a thumbs-up to this being a solid old building, designed to last.

On your way in, to underline it all, you might like to take a little detour through the gym. There are windows there through which you can climb and end up on a tiny balcony right at the top of the building, above the second L of 'COUNTY HALL'. The view is breathtaking – it's the most famous stretch of the Thames, with some of its most iconic buildings, from the aforementioned Eye, right across to the Houses of Parliament.

The view across the Thames to the Houses of Parliament.

OASIS SPORTS CENTRE

What luck: a fabulous minute-long British Pathé newsreel from 1954 all about the Oasis Sports Centre. It describes, in those precise tones beloved of public-information films of the era, 'an unexpected little world of sandcastles and sunshine, sandwiches and swimming'. It tells how the pool was built on a bombsite by an 'inspired borough council' and calls it 'a fashionable haven for typists and tycoons alike; resting actresses, bearded bohemians and not-so-busy housewives and pavement-weary shoppers'. The categories may feel as dated as the plummy voice and swirly strings music, and the pool surroundings bear little resemblance to what exists today (there's no sandpit, for starters). But the film ends with 'it really is an oasis', and that remains the same; a hidden gem, easy to miss, just off the busy streets between Holborn and Covent Garden.

The outdoor pool (there is also a 25m indoor pool, a calmer, quieter space where dappled light plays on the shabby décor) is now cramped on all sides by the leisure centre building and by a low-rise block of flats whose brick walkways face the water – my inner daredevil reckons it must be very tempting to leap off into the pool after closing time on a hot summer's night. It means you get less sky, just a square of it directly overhead. The pool surround is a little crowded with functional storage boxes; there's been a half-hearted attempt to tart it up with a couple of plant pots but it certainly doesn't have the sense of being somewhere you might lounge around in glamorous 1950s swimwear eating sandwiches in your lunch hour. The pool is now only 27m and heated to within an inch of its life, except where the pool depth drops and you hit a slightly colder

If shopping and opera aren't your thing, just north of Covent Garden is an Oasis.

If the outdoor pool is full to capacity, the indoor pool is a welcome alternative.

The Oasis is a well-known place for watching the world go by.

patch. On that deep-end wall are three huge underwater conical steel lights, surely modelled on Madonna's bra cup circa *Vogue*.

If there's something in the comparison – how it was in that brief black-and-white clip from 1954 with how it is now – that gives one pause for thought, then it is the enviable beauty of men diving from the original high board and the fat-faced baby doggie-paddling determinedly across the water; the sense of freedom and happiness, right here, in this pool, in the heart of the capital. It maybe has as much to do with their carefree insouciance playing against our own grouchy sense of entitlement as it does the 'improved' environs. Yes, of course we have more stuff – refurbished changing rooms with plenty of hairdryers – and we're marginally better on gender stereotyping. But they seem happier! So we should do as they appear on film to be doing: cherishing, absolutely in the moment, the bliss of being in an outdoor pool right in the heart of town.

Oasis Sports Centre

Address 32 Endell Street, Covent Garden, London WC2H 9AG
Phone 0207 831 1804
Web www.better.org.uk/leisure/oasis-sports-centre

KENTISH TOWN SPORTS CENTRE

If anyone needs a lesson in how best to restore old baths, then this is the pool to visit. It is an utterly splendid Grade II listed testament to what is possible in our architectural heritage.

Just off Kentish Town High Street on a corner, is a huge red-brick gothic Edwardian building. It stands its ground majestically, and it's only when you crane your neck up to look beyond the cliff face that you see the glint of a glass triangle roof hidden up there, hinting at newer additions within. The original pool entrance, tastefully painted doors with the words 'Public Hall' in gilded letters above, is now the entrance to flats; the discreetly designed new pool entrance is on a side street called Inkerman Road.

The reception area and separate changing rooms are nice enough; it's when you go through to Willes Pool (past a 25m pool with two shallow ends, so perfect for teaching) that the real delights reveal themselves. The way in through two huge dark-wood doors feels like you're being called to the boardroom. Then there's the pool. This is where the really successful lesson in mixing old and new begins.

Beautifully restored, with fabulous detail, it's a perfectly proportioned pool.

Firstly, the colour scheme. You can fancy it up by calling it 'elephant breath' or 'mushroom gill' – it's definitely beige. The walls are tiled in it, with a soft blue/grey tile line. The key word is 'subtle'. There are subtle rounds of lighting in the roof of the balcony area which runs round three sides; above is a stunning restored ceiling of arched plasterwork with, above that again, a long domed window. Great chunky wooden window frame structures play brilliantly against the delicacy of the painted plaster. At the deep end, there's a church-like arched window with sculpted leaf detail in sandblasted orange terracotta. The level of detailing, so perfectly restored, is glorious.

The central jewel is the pool itself, the original 'first-class men's pool'. The first-class men of the 1900s obviously had high expectations; this is 33m long, and the all-round depth is excellent: there's no scraping your knees on the bottom of the shallow end and the deep end is good for a standing dive. There's quite a drop between the edge of the pool and the water itself as there's inbuilt guttering; and the water is at a temperature that keeps you moving. So if you get nothing else from this, if you couldn't give a hoot for fine restoration detail or subtle colourways, you'll have a good swim.

It's only when you get out that you realise what it hasn't got. It hasn't got garish signage, or hysterical depth notices every two centimetres, or paraphernalia scattered everywhere. So all you see is the detail shining through, which turns this into a haven, a retreat. And that's a real achievement.

Don't forget to spend five minutes in the gallery enjoying the quality of the place.

Kentish Town Sports Centre

Address Grafton Road, Kentish Town, London NW5 3DU
Phone 0207 974 7000
Web www.better.org.uk/leisure/kentish-town-sports-centre

HAMPSTEAD PONDS

The challenge here is not a swimming one. The challenge here is to encapsulate in a few words a place that really merits an entire book.* These historic, iconic ponds have been written about many times before but, like a glamorous olden-days film star, they manage to be famous yet feel quite secret. What they have is enigmatic, hard to quantify, and can only really be understood by experiencing the ponds first-hand.

The mystique of the ponds is built from very ordinary materials. The spluttering outdoor showers are cold. The changing rooms are like deserted cowsheds. The simple platforms for entering the water are made from old wood and functional grey metal poles. State of the art it is not. But these basic things in the context of this heath have become something plainly extraordinary, something that feels like another world.

Hampstead Heath, an ancient green land of paths and hills and woods and aimless wandering, has three swimmable ponds: separate men's and women's ponds towards the northeast of the Heath, open to the public all year, and a mixed pond down in the southwest corner open from May to September. They have been swum in for hundreds of years by champions, tourists and ordinary Londoners brought together by their love of being out in the open air and the fresh water, surrounded by trees and reeds, with the possibility of a kingfisher flashing past or the grey ghost of a heron overhead.

It isn't quite true that the challenge is not a swimming one: the water is cold and brackish, your hands become almost invisible as they slide ahead of you in the olive green. And 'secret', too, might be disingenuous; the ponds can be packed on a blue-sky day – but there's a 'no kids under

It's hard to believe, looking at this picture, that Oxford Street is only 20 minutes away.

eight' rule. There are precautionary signs up on hypothermia, but there's no official guidance on how to deter nosy coots or jumping carp – a certain amount of respect is required. There is no visibility here, no lines to follow on the bottom of the pool, no certainty about what's directly under your feet. And swimming with that uncertainty, an apprehension, almost fear, of what might brush your skin, is as adrenaline-inducing as the cold water.

History inevitably brings politics, and there is plenty of both here. The history includes great photos of early Victorian bathing, tales of men lining the banks of the women's pond to watch the 'modern Spartans' bathe. The politics are sexual, local and financial: swimming here used to be free but now costs £2, and in the past there has been hysterical reporting about gay activity and the covering of nipples (female) at the single-sex pools. And our own modern Spartans, the swimmers who break the ice here for winter dips, still attract open-mouthed attention, mostly revolving around the word 'why'.

* I said it was a challenge to encapsulate these ponds in a few words, but there's a bench at the mixed pond that does it in five. Inscribed for Jimmy McIvor it says, 'This is dreamy swimming here'. Indeed it is.

* see bibliography.

A sanctuary, a holiday or a retreat, Hampstead Ponds is one of London's greatest assets.

Hampstead Ponds

Address Hampstead Heath, London NW3
Phone 0207 485 3873
Web www.cityoflondon.gov.uk/things-to-do/green-spaces/hampstead-heath/swimming/Pages/default.aspx

LONDON FIELDS LIDO

Every time you go for a swim here, one of two year-round 50m heated outdoor pools in London since the reopening of Charlton Lido, please remember a few individuals to whose extraordinary tenacity this pool is testament. They are the ones who literally stopped the bulldozers demolishing the existing building by standing in the way, who ceaselessly campaigned, lobbied and challenged, who garnered local, city, even national support, who showed that individuals can make a difference. To those people, every time I cross London Fields and see the low red-brick building in the corner, I say a small but heartfelt 'thank you'.

Because for a long time this lido looked like a lost cause. Opened in 1932 on the crest of a lido wave, it closed in 1988 when indoor leisure centres and private gyms became fashionable. The years that followed saw the place almost demolished, squatted in, and generally neglected and overgrown. After the aforementioned battles, it opened again in its current incarnation in October 2006, and since then outdoor swimming has hit a boom. We're back riding a wave of lido love and this is a choice place to do it.

You wouldn't actually get much of a clue there was a pool inside from the exterior: it just looks like a long, flat institution, albeit a kindly one. There's a modern entrance and corridors to changing rooms. These are functional; the pool is very well used so it's often a polite nudge-and-budge process in the limited space. And bring flip-flops: when padding out across the

Since it re-opened in 2006, London Fields Lido has attracted outdoor swimmers from every corner of the capital and beyond.

paving slabs to shove your bag in a locker, if the ground is cold your feet will be too. The lockers provide a splash of primary colour in what is essentially a massive brick courtyard, with the pool taking up almost the whole centre. There's only space at one end for a few sunbathers, the other three sides have narrow walkways. It's further enclosed by modern steel hand railings; but because the building is low we get a lot of borrowed view from over the walls. At one end, nice Victorian villas; on another side, a large old school and tower blocks hover. Although there are sturdy old trees visible on all sides, it feels quintessentially urban but very protected, everything wrapping round us warmly.

The 50m pool has a walk-in entry or standard steps, and the lanes are generous with plenty of overtaking space. And although it's heated, it's kept to the lower end of acceptable – once you're in you need to keep moving, so it's not really a play space. The depth drops gradually, and it is infinity-edged, so it's a fast pool, fast enough, indeed, to have been the only London lido to have played host to training the 2012 Olympic swimmers. Being open all year round offers some great opportunities – when an unheated swim feels too challenging and an indoor swim too dull, this is the best choice. On a cold day you can relish swimming into the steam rising from the water's surface.

Lovingly restored and beautifully maintained, the lanes are generous with plenty of overtaking space.

London Fields Lido

Address London Fields West Side, Hackney,
London E8 3EU
Phone 0207 254 9038
Web www.hackney.gov.uk/c-londonfields-lido.htm

PARLIAMENT HILL LIDO

Cold-water swimmers of north London are lucky – they have a choice. There's Parliament Hill Lido, North London's only year-round heated Lido. Or, as the lido sits right at the bottom of the Heath, there's Hampstead Ponds, a more 'natural' alternative, although most people would argue that there's nothing natural about breaking the ice on a cold January morning for a freezing dip. At 61m (200 feet) Parliament Hill is not the largest unheated lido in London – that accolade goes to the 91m Tooting Lido – but it does have the shiniest bottom.

The architectural heritage here is obvious, particularly if you've already studied Brockwell Lido, which had the same architects, and opened a year before in the summer of 1937. In the 1930s they built long and low; this is a one-storey, letterbox-windowed red-brick face, with the word 'LIDO' set out in time-appropriate font. There are newer exit and entrance ramps right and left but apart from them and the metal mesh covering the windows, it looks pretty much as it

The steel lining of Parliament Hill Lido gives the water a very particular hue.

must have done back in the day. The same can be said once you clunk through the turnstile. State of the art it is not. And all the better for that.

Out through some heavy plastic draught-excluder strips, the pool is enclosed by the building, but with generous margins for sunbathing, a café and a typical 1930s layer-cake fountain. There's a rickety slide on one side but, alas, the old diving boards have gone the way of most diving boards. Deck-edged, it is lined in stainless steel so is essentially a massive sink; from the top that gives the water a grey tinge. Stainless steel is more common as a pool liner in Europe, though still rare in the UK. Underwater, it has a lovely brightness; plus it keeps its pristine looks. It is patterned with welds and raised

There are a hardy bunch of winter swimmers, but while the water is cold, the welcome won't be.

buttons, pleasingly tactile, and it doesn't feel like a cold material, which is surprising given the context. The shallow end is very shallow – as you front-crawl up to it, you can watch the

Parliament Hill Lido

Address Gordon House Road, London NW5 1NB
Phone 0207 485 3873
Web www.cityoflondon.gov.uk/things-to-do/green-spaces/hampstead-heath/swimming/Pages/default.aspx

bubbles under your hands flatten on the floor then scuttle behind you like escaping jellyfish. Getting in is quite difficult – you have to wade quite a way before you're waist deep, and of course there is the cold to contend with.

While the pool feels steel-sleek-modern, the changing facilities here would make a cow feel at home. The women's is a barn: cold floor, metal ceiling, open cubicles in thick primary red, yellow and blue paint. It can feel fairly brutal even on a sunny day, but it chimes with the simplicity of the whole place. There are no fancy accessories like hairdryers or heaters apart from one small heater high on the wall that might eventually warm the top of your head if you stood beneath it all day. The message is clear: if you need wrapping in cotton wool after you've dipped, bring your own.

DAVID LLOYD FINCHLEY

The least appealing thing about swimming here is also the thing that will confront you first: the location. There's no disguising the fact that it is part of a soulless complex of big hangar-style stores where parking is king. Hopefully, your glass is half full: parking is available.

Unless this is your first experience of a private gym, the décor in the changing rooms will be familiar. Grey stone-tiled floor, dark-wood lockers, square benches to change on, lots of mirrors and hairdryers. There's the perennial padlock conundrum to get around (the conundrum being if you're short-sighted and put your glasses in your bag while you swim, you'll struggle to see the numbers on your padlock when you come to undo it). There's a generous sense of space though, even down to the showers, which are bigger than absolutely necessary, so you don't feel that everything's thoughtlessly crammed in.

Through to the indoor pool. Under a triangular corrugated roof, it's 20m in length, with two square Jacuzzi pools hitched to the side, but lanes wide enough for overtaking. The room feels like a modestly converted barn, with one wall of simple sliding doors to the fields outside. Actually, it doesn't open out onto fields but they've made efforts with the space, even if it is a bit of a mishmash. There are bits of screening here and there, scrappy roofs and hedging, little paved areas leading to other little paved areas, palm trees, a tennis court, views of massive inflatable rooms. It's like walking behind the scenes in a garden centre, but the outdoor pool is the key to

Watching the steam rise on a cold, misty morning is a perfect start to any day.

While there's less space inside, there's plenty on offer for the less intrepid swimmer.

being here so keep your focus on that – the rest is literally just background.

You flip-flop up some stairs and across paving slabs to get to the pool – a sometimes chilly 30-second 'journey' that, surprisingly, plenty of people don't bother with. What they are missing is a full 25m pool. The lanes are narrower so if it's busy (which it can be first thing in the morning) it may be a little testing. However, it is heated but not to boiling point, and if you catch the right weather conditions you'll get that lovely light steam coming off the surface, which, when a grey mizzling day meets a blue misted pool, can be very photogenic. Once you're in the water, you see that the paving slab edges are a little unforgiving, the pool lining a little tired and there's sand on the bottom (from the filter system, so it is meant to be there). The pool is 1.2m deep throughout, but the edge is lipped so don't expect your fastest times, but it's a great antidote to the 'fake heat' of an indoor swim and to the feeling of being stuck in a car, which you are most likely to have been, to get here. The pool has limited opening hours in winter months, but still, plenty of heated outdoor pools only open in the summer, which seems the wrong way round.

David Lloyd Finchley

Address Leisure Way, High Road, Finchley, London N12 0QZ
Phone 0845 129 6791
Web www.davidlloyd.co.uk/home/clubs/finchley/opening

CROUCH END LIDO

Crouch End has become shorthand for a very particular kind of boiled wool middle-class stereotype. 'It's like a village!' people proudly proclaim as they drive their electric cars to the nearest tube station. So you'd imagine the lido would be a macrobiotic affair and, indeed, the front of the building has been wood-clad, which is architect shorthand for modern trend. But beyond that facade, it's a different story. If it was an island, it would be Canvey.

The lido is part of Park Road Leisure Centre so there are indoor and diving pools on site, open year-round while the lido is seasonal (May to September). The indoor pools certainly wouldn't warrant their own space on a '50 best' list, but their ceiling design may get on a '50 most odd'. The ticketing arrangement means you have to pick one or the other, but the decision is a no-brainer: choose outside.

There are not nearly enough 50m outdoor pools in London. In the light of that, quirks are easily excused. And this lido has plenty of those. For a start, the wooden cladding at the front gives way to ridged red metal round the back, which makes you feel like you're swimming in a container park. There are trimmed Leylandii all round the perimeter (the tree equivalent of the breeze block), sad little firs in half-barrel planters at irregular intervals, and the pool is over-signed – five clunky exhortations on one narrow grass strip alone. There's an outdated red line painted right round the edge of the

While only open in the summer, Crouch End offers an excellent sized pool at the perfect temperature.

pool that visually jars with the water's blue. The loos are in a portacabin which makes everything feel temporary and the paving looks a bit out of sorts.

There is plenty of room to picnic after your swim, and the showers are outdoor too.

And then, quirks forgotten, there is the good stuff. It's great to prolong being outside after a swim, with outdoor showers and lounging opportunities on a grassy slope. The pool sits central to this, well proportioned, nicely wide and, unusually, shallow at both ends and deeper in the middle, which can confuse your swimming rhythm somewhat. There is a small children's pool to one side so you may get the whole space uninterrupted by play, but sometimes they lane off the ends, leaving the

middle to do circular laps in. Mostly, it's left joyfully free-form. Yes, it is a bit knackered and cracked on the bottom, but it's a great length and when the tiniest cloud appears, there's plenty of space. It's also, uniquely among the city's outdoor pools, heated to between 17 and 20 degrees 'depending on weather conditions'. Usually, pools are either heated to 25 degrees or above, or are unheated; you can call this a halfway compromise or you can call it a kind gesture. It means the bite of the water may be less painfully crisp, but it's not so warm that it feels like dipping in mulled wine. It won't please a purist, but here we're all looking beyond the quirks, cherishing instead the too-rare beauty of outdoor swimming.

Park Road Leisure Centre

Address
Park Road, Hornsey, London N8 8JN

Phone
0208 341 3567

Web
www.fusion-lifestyle.com

YORK HALL LEISURE CENTRE

Is a pool's heritage enough to tempt a person to commend their almost-naked body to the waters? Sometimes it has to be. Given the choice between it and the pristine London Fields Lido a mere bus ride away, I know which I'd go for. So what warrants this pool's inclusion?

Firstly, the history, sporting and otherwise. You might already be familiar with the name 'York Hall' – it is, after all, one of the most famous boxing venues in the country. Originally opened in 1929 by the Duke of York, it had a famous Turkish bath, steam and vapour rooms in the basement, and two pools. There's now just one, with a small baby pool add-on, built in the 1960s and refurbished in the early 2000s. You'd be hard pushed to spot the refurbishment; it's distinctly shabby outside and in.

The history is obvious from the outside: the solid red-brick neo-Georgian building, the balcony, then the tall traditional railings, painted a garish 'job lot' red and green, strike a discordant note. Doors blocked with metal concertina shutters and outdated entrance signs add to the air of neglect.

Inside, there's a grander entrance hall painted in a municipal sherbet green, and robust corridors to the changing rooms, which are big but basic – I should warn you that the mirror in the ladies' changing area is a funfair joke, making even the slenderest twig look fat and squat. But then, round the corner, it all opens up in front of you, a massive space – my swimming companion told me it's like when you go to a football match and crest the stadium stairs and there, ahead, is the view of the pitch and sky and crowd.

York Hall is one of the few pools with the diving boards still intact.

It's a really cheering sight, the light at the end of the tunnel. And it is this that warrant's York Hall's inclusion.

This was actually Britain's first pool to measure 33-and-a-bit metres long; it's proportionately wide, without the need of funfair-mirror trickery. At one end is a gigantic wall of permanently steamed-up windows with concrete chevrons as per the 1960s heritage. And in front of that, a glorious diving board standing over the water like an oversized horseshoe crab guarding a rock pool. The height of the board guarantees that the deep end is very deep, which just increases the sense of space. The pool also has raised edges, which makes for a slow swim, because movement makes the water choppy, and that chop has nowhere to go but back into the pool. It is slow, but lovely, with a pleasing cool tactility to the rounded marble ends. They may be cracked and old but it's better to keep your eyes on them and the water, rather than looking up to the tatty plastic-seated environs, or the garish blue-strutted ceiling.

If you need more than size and history to tempt you, the old Turkish baths are now a spa, its entrance delineated by that quintessentially modern touch, scented candles.

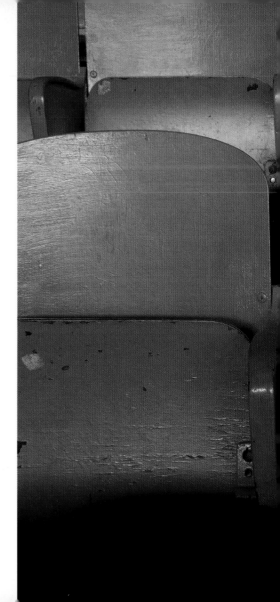

The original features provide a sense of York Hall's unique history as a swimming and boxing complex.

York Hall Leisure Centre

Address
5 Old Ford Road, Bethnal Green, London E2 9PJ
Phone
0208 980 2243
Web
www.better.org.uk/leisure/york-hall-leisure-centre

CANARY RIVERSIDE CLUB

Question: how do you write about James Bond when you've never seen a James Bond film and don't want to resort to 'shaken not stirred' clichés? Answer: you use the word 'apparently' a lot. So: apparently, this pool is in the Bond film, *Skyfall;* apparently, Daniel Craig swims in it; apparently, it's in Shanghai. So apparently, if you follow the laws of homeopathy, by swimming in it you become a little bit Daniel Craig (though obviously it's not just homeopaths who'd want that).

There's no doubt: knowing you're in a pool where Daniel Craig has swum does rub off a little – you might find yourself pulling your shoulders back, sucking your belly in. The glamour of it all is underlined by a sign in the changing area: 'No Paparazzi!' which is slightly self-defeating if it never even occurred to you to have a gander at anyone else in there. This area is tasteful, if not exactly top drawer, though the lockers are not friendly to those of us who lock our glasses away when we swim. (In fairness, Canary Riverside isn't the only pool where this problem occurs.)

The view from the pool might be familiar to anyone who had seen the James Bond film, *Skyfall*.

The route to the pool is lined with quiet areas exhorting you to 'relax and unwind' in various watering holes hot and bubbly. Stairs go up to the main attraction – and yes, the pool room is stunning. It's essentially a superbly scaled great big box, with massive glass walls. The floor is decked, worn to just the right degree; the ceiling and the huge plain columns at each corner are similarly wood-clad, giving a warm and stylish look. One side is abutted by a grass area and the windows of what looks like a generic new-build hotel, another looks out to the lead-clad gym block. But this is not what makes swimming here such a spectacular experience. From the other side the pool looks out over the Thames, giving you the feeling of being suspended above the river. It is a fantastic view of the capital. Because it's on the first floor, you are eye-level with newish trees on the walkway below, but they've been pushed to the sides so as not to obscure the view as they grow. There are few experiences in London to match standing in your swimming costume and counting off all the sites, though you'd do well to remember the passing boats who might treat you, in your swimming attire, as one of the city's newest sights.

The actual pool only just takes second place. It is small at 20m, but it's an infinity pool, and the same depth all along (1.2m) and laned, to underline that you're here to swim, not just to

The sensation of being suspended above the Thames, combined with the views, makes swimming here an unforgettable experience.

pleasure-bob while staring out at the massive sky and the constantly changing river. Everything round the pool is tasteful, too: the graceful curves of the steel handrails, the solid loungers around it, everything as modern and cool as our premier fictional spy has ever been.

If it's good enough for James Bond, it is certainly good enough for me. Don't go to pretend you're in Shanghai, though. From up here, there's no doubt we're in the heart of the capital.

Canary Riverside Health Club

Address West Ferry Circus, Canary Wharf, London E14 8RR
Phone 0207 513 2999
Web www.virginactive.co.uk/clubs/canary-riverside

WALTHAMSTOW FOREST COLLEGE POOL

If you know this pool you may look quizzically at its inclusion here; it's certainly more beast than beauty. And, like that tale, its story is also about not judging on superficial looks, and about other things too. About standing for something, the power of community, about passion and politics. That's a lot of stories for one swimming pool in E17, but sometimes it's good to be reminded of what 'standing for something' can achieve.

At the top of a grand sweep of steps is the six-pillared entrance to Walthamstow Forest College, the big old beast of a building completed in 1939. The grandeur doesn't continue inside; the door to the basement changing rooms looks like you could be going into a classroom on a long school corridor. Beyond the door, tiny cubicles (barely enlivened by striped plastic curtains as doors) and cold showers in a big trough don't set a great mood.

The pool itself is set in a plain room, which in other circumstances might be a shabby post-war church hall. The square-framed windows hang right underneath the square-tiled ceiling. This is an unadorned but chunky 30m pool with a cloudy bottom that looks like someone unsuccessfully applied white paint on top of black. You can just make out '3'6' in faded red on the shallow end. The bottom of the pool feels like it was once gritty, but has been worn down by busy feet. It also feels hot: it's hard to hide a new temperature gauge when the bright red of a digital readout is so incongruous in these otherwise unembellished surroundings.

A satisfyingly chunky pool, well-used by local community groups.

Because of the colour of the pool and everything it reflects, the water doesn't have that crisp contemporary blue; it looks a little greenish almost. It's an 'old-fashioned', almost 1950s look, and feel. The whole place has it. A sombre row of tatty white plastic chairs interrupted by two blue ones make a splendid study for some photo realism.

The pool is only accessible at limited times when it opens for a 'community swim'. It's on the radar for swim clubs, but a bit of a well-kept secret, even locally; it's not obvious from outside the building, it's not part of a chain, it doesn't have a massive budget for any kind of advertising. That's explained by the next bit of the story.

Five years ago, Waltham Forest College announced that their pool was not 'key to delivery of services' and decided to shut it. Local people stepped up and started a 'Friends of the Pool' group. This group eventually persuaded the local council to get involved, but the arrangement was short-lived and at the end of 2009 the pool was closed. The 'Friends of the Pool' did not give up and for six months paid to

Volunteers saved this pool from certain closure - one day there might be a plaque to commemerate them.

keep the closed pool ticking over so it didn't fall into ruin. That admirable approach paid off as the pool was reopened in April 2010; a regeneration company temporarily ran it while a not-for-profit Community Interest Company was set up and a thirty-year lease negotiated. The Community Pool was born! Two hundred thousand pounds was raised for a new plant room, air-handling units and a pool cover: practical concerns that reduced the running costs by a third. The college still owns the freehold for the site – it's built into the integral fabric of the building – but the lease is now owned and the facility is run by The Community Pool CIC as a completely separate business.

That this pool is up and running is testament to a bunch of local folk. People with will and effort and the passion for an ordinary place. As members of a swimming community, we tip our swim hats in gratitude.

Walthamstow Forest College

Address Walthamstow Forest College, 707 Forest Road, London E17 4JB
Phone 0208 521 7192
Web thecommunitypool.org

VIRGIN ACTIVE REPTON PARK

What I have tried to do in this book is impart a little of what it's like to swim in each featured pool. In this case, there's an added complication, because here the task is to impart what it's like to swim in a church . . .

About 50 metres before a road sign proclaiming a 'Welcome to Essex' is a huge pair of iron gates to Repton Park, described as a 'gated village community' built on the site of the old Claybury Asylum. It mixes old buildings and new along neat 'boulevards', and the institution's former chapel has been converted into a members-only gym.

This being a 'branded' gym, it does all the accoutrements in the changing rooms well: heaps of towels, plenty of space, nicely decked-out toilets and showers (though sitting in the sauna feels like sitting in a hot shop window). The lighting is low, the stone tiling, of which there's a lot, is moody, and the lockers are dark wood, each one like an old piece of panelling. It's entirely possible to imagine a choirboy neatly hanging up his cassock here. The aim is an atmosphere of quiet calm, the result maybe a tad confessional, but that's where personal experience and feelings about church come in (it's impossible, I would suggest, to keep them out).

It's almost a shame to go any further with descriptions because it makes such a good surprise. However, the double doors to the pool are also dark wood, with arched windows – they must be original. You go through and, yes, it's an actual church, a very well-preserved one at that. But of course it's not a church, because in the central nave, where the aisle and seats would

It's not every day that you get to swim in a former church.

Light, glorious and beautiful, this is a swimming experience to remember.

be, there's a pool: A lovely, light, clean 24m pool. It's a bizarre, and glorious, yet slightly strange and definitely discombobulating sight.

It's also beautiful. Huge pillars line up alongside the pool, all the brickwork meticulously restored so it looks pristine; there's a massive stained-glass window at one end and stained glass in small arched windows down each side. It lets in a particular kind of light, almost dancing thick with colour. The ceiling is huge, wooden, arched; simple circular metal light fittings hang overhead

on long, long chains. There's an apse at the deep end (a semi-circular addition to the rectangular main room) that has a sunken hydro pool where the pulpit would have been, and beyond that, in place of an altar, a stand-alone shower built of glass bricks. The altar/shower hides a small seated area behind, for secret skiving.

So what's it really like to swim in a church? Do surroundings make a difference? For me, it appears that a lifetime of forced genuflection has a residual impact; it feels contemplative and respectful. But that may disappear on repetition and, I suspect, during thumping-loud aquafit sessions. In any case, when your head is down and you're clocking up the lengths, all you see is a nice block of a pool. It's only in your imagination that you might be nervously laughing at the thought of scampering up the aisle in your bathers.

Virgin Active Repton Park

Address Manor Road, Woodford Spa, Essex IG8 8GN
Phone 0208 506 6300
Web www.virginactive.co.uk/clubs/repton-park

KING'S OAK LIDO

We are right on the western edge of the ancient woodland of Epping Forest, the city's largest open space at over 6,000 acres, teetering on the northeast edge of London. Although it's within the M25, it's Essex really. A few minutes ago you were slap-bang in the madness of busy traffic lanes and roundabouts with too many options. Moments later, you were on lanes shaded by arching trees; now you are here, Paul's Nursery Road, where, with the pub behind you, there is an amazing view across the north of our city.

The phrase 'with the pub behind you' is a navigational guide, not a suggestion that you visit one before you swim. You don't need to anyway, because this lido is situated in the grounds of a large pub, the King's Oak, in a village called High Beech (or sometimes Beach), the only settlement within Epping Forest and called High because it's 110m above sea level, hence the great views.

It's a unique scenario because water and alcohol don't usually make natural companions. It's unique too in that this was once a public lido and is now private; a public house is self-evidently free to enter, but the pool is not – you have to pay a day fee or get family or individual membership, from April all the way through to October (if it's an Indian summer).

Set in the pub's back garden, the lido is a 1930s original with an architectural style that is a little at odds with the more modern overdressed trimmings that surround it. Complete with the cascading tiered fountain

Right on the edge of Epping Forest, what was once public space is now part of a pub.

that would be familiar to visitors to Tooting, Parliament Hill and Uxbridge Lidos, it's 100ft long – that's just over 30m – rectangle of that very particular blue, with a white edge and a proper deep end. It's been well looked after, and is in excellent condition. There are integral steps into the shallow end, the sides have guttered hand-grabs, and the water is unheated. It's surrounded by numerous lounging opportunities, though the pub itself seems to be creeping ever nearer, with a variety of chandeliered tent areas. On one side are trees, and there's a curved white wall beyond the deep end, although the peep-holes in it only offer a view out to the car park. Under the green leaf canopy, a small thatched round hut serves as an outdoor bar. Meanwhile, the changing rooms are sheds. They are painted and

Some of the Lido features are very familiar, but rarely do they come with such poolside service.

It's easy to come for a swim and end up spending the whole day here.

nicely maintained, but still undoubtedly garden sheds, one women's, one gents'. Tiled floors, a toilet and sink . . . neat but rudimentary, and no shower facilities so don't rely on hot water to warm you up again afterwards. You have to exit these sheds and tiptoe cautiously across some white gravel to the pool, so bring flip-flops and a warm layer to wrap up in afterwards. Alternatively, the forest is a Site of Special Scientific Interest, and a power walk is a good way to warm up after a cold swim.

In the old days, the glory days of London lidos, this pool was one of several in the area – including two giants, Whipps Cross Lido and Larkswood Open Air Pool, both of which met their final demise in the 1980s. King's Oak is the only survivor.

King's Oak Hotel

Address
Paul's Nursery Road,
High Beach, Essex
IG10 4AE
Phone
0208 508 5000
Web wildswim.com

AQUATICS CENTRE

At the time of writing this pool was a building site, being turned from Olympic venue into a major public swimming one, and I was honoured to get the opportunity to visit the work-in-progress. So rather than an exploration of what it's like to swim here, this is a eulogy to a building. The Aquatics Centre should be open to the public in 2014.

And what a building. For many people, memories of it are tied in with that glorious Olympic and Paralympic summer of 2012, and in that sense it already has an emotional heritage – one of exalting in achievement. It left us awe-inspired and fortified, bound into community, however temporarily.

The Centre, designed by internationally recognised architect Zaha Hadid, was nicknamed the Stingray because of the way the roof looks like a ray in full flowing movement buoyed by water. Massive glass walls replace the now-removed extra Olympic seating wings, though there's still plenty of gallery space. Two huge contemporary entrance halls, one upper, one lower, all glass and steel and concrete surfaces, lead through to the main attractions: not one, but two 50m swimming pools.

The known practicalities first: both pools are infinity edged, with booms to change the size and moving floors to change the depth. The main pool is 3m deep throughout with racing ends. Backstage, there are 13 massive filter systems, so the chlorine levels are minimal. And because this is part of our Olympic legacy, it's not going to be exorbitantly priced, rather it will be in line with other local facilities.

The first 50m pool, the training pool, was where the athletes warmed up and

Set to become one of the most iconic images of post-Olympic London.

down. It's in a huge hall with polished concrete-block walls – these are the Aquatic Centre's signature piece, the flaws a part of its living beauty. The distinctive low ceiling has regimented cut-outs graduating from slits to petal shapes – think Middle Eastern design – filled with a frosted light, and there are tiled shallow bench niches. Everything is neutral, simple, pared; the colours are warm like the sun just went down. At one end, the glass wall lets onto the main hall – a blue slab of brightness beyond.

From this blocky, low-lit intense space you go to the main pool hall, which floods your eyes with its scale and light. This is a celebration of nature, of form, in vibrant slopes and curves. This is the jewel. The hall is enormous, the scale fantastic, swimmers little more than tiny specks on the water. The ceiling is a massive wave, or the underside of a whale, fluid and graceful; light wells sit like barnacles. Bright and cavernous, but not empty, there is real warmth coming from the organic shapes,

and nothing feels straight except the pool, which sits centre stage. At one end, a separate diving pool with the famous diving boards. And they are beautiful. Precast concrete rising from the ground, bowing into integrated boards, like parts of a mammoth skeleton pushing up through sand. Put your hand on these works of art and tell me this isn't national heritage. This is a monument to the great achievements of 2012, and now it's ours. Truly, we are blessed.

Glamorous and exciting, it is an architectural wonder both inside and out.

Aquatics Centre

Address Queen Elizabeth Olympic Park, London E20 2ZQ
Web www.better.org.uk

WEST RESERVOIR, STOKE NEWINGTON

Stoke Newington – out on the urban edge, where hipsters migrate to breed – might not spring to mind as a likely open-water swim venue. But actually, in the not too distant past, Stoke Newington's reservoirs were an integral part of London's water supply, and only became defunct in the 1990s, at which point they were handed to the borough to provide recreation facilities. So this is just the next chapter in Stoke Newington's watery history.

Green Lanes N4, behind what was a pumping station designed in the 1850s to look like a Scottish castle and is now a climbing centre, is our destination. Down a lane to a great square tower – the original four-storey filtration station, a red block with light brick banding and tall windows – with new wings attached on either side. As you arrive, you get two great views. Ahead, through the windows, is the lake itself, right across to the tree boundaries and the tower blocks and cranes beyond. The other view is up, into the mechanisms, elegant but substantial, a paean to a working building of the old sort. All very tastefully renovated, with two cast plates embedded in the floor glorifying water. And this is what we've come for.

Lakes and good facilities: the two things don't normally go hand in hand. Here they do, because there is space. The changing rooms are generous, the showers warm and there are plenty of lockers. Out on the hardwood jetties that provide a great viewing platform, if that's all you can bring yourself to do (there's a decent café too), you get a sense of how urban this setting really

One of the newest venues for open-water training in the capital.

is. Tower blocks look over from all sides and just behind the screen of trees, cranes spider up from the horizon – from up top the swimmers would be merely tiny shining black dots imperceptibly moving to a beat of silver-mercury splashes. And then it's down to the water's edge. Here, it's a jump or slide off the edge and in. Before you enter the water, find your sighting spot (the small buoy right up the other end is low, and takes a while to hove into view, so I chose a tree). If it's cold then take a few minutes to get your breathing under control. Once you've done that you'll notice that the water quality is excellent, sharp, clear and dark with specks of green fluorescence flowing round you like someone shook out a moss blanket.

A full lap of the lake is 750m, and the first leg is the longest, and not just because it takes a while to fully acclimatise. From there the route takes you round the curve (the course is a backward D) and then home for as many times as you can handle. Take care not to cut off the final corner too early, as you'd just be cheating yourself of an exhilarating outdoor swimming experience, as well as getting an unusually quick time that you'll have to explain to your fellow swimmers. The exit is then up a slippery concrete path. A useful tip I can pass on is that it's quicker to crawl up it rather than try to stand, fall, and end up crawling anyway. Once you're out you can quickly pad through the main hall again to the bliss of a good shower.

The old water station has been given a renewed lease of life.

West Reservoir Water Sports Centre

Address Green Lanes, Hackney, London N4 2HA
Phone 0208 442 8116
Web www.better.org.uk

KING'S HALL LEISURE CENTRE
AND CLISSOLD LEISURE CENTRE

Two pools geographically close, but about as different as it's possible for two swimming baths to be. Ten minutes and about a hundred years apart.

First, to King's Hall, where 'faded' is a kind description indeed. It's a Grade II listed once-magnificent confection of a building crammed indelicately on a busy, too-narrow pavement; as sad as Miss Haversham's wedding cake. Inside it's structurally substantial: old parquet flooring echoing down wide sturdy corridors. There appear to be two entrances, male and female, but both doors lead to the same changing area with banks of modern lockers and a newish shower block that suggest work has been done. The pool hall has an A-shaped, wired-glass roof, the glass painted nicotine yellow; there's a children's pool and a 25m swimming pool in familiar crackled white-brick tile. Two vast and clanging air-conditioning units thunder away on the tatty balcony; three huge frosted-plastic windows that look like oversized washing-machine doors are set in one wall. If places reflect us, this one is for old and scruffy folk.

So why even include it in this book? Because of what this pool was, what it is, what it could be. It was, it is, our heritage. That's so important. You can feel the history. It's fatigued, but it could be beautiful again – I've seen these pools restored, some of them are in this book, they are fabulous. We have to swim here – yes, have to – otherwise, it may go. If they pulled it

A Grade II listed building, King's Hall represents a key landmark in London's rich swimming heritage.

down, that would be terrible. It is perfectly possible to have a training swim here, but these are not competition conditions. So instead, you could swim differently, consciously, look around and picture Hackney folk flocking here in 1897 . . . feel grateful for what we have.

It's not hysteria to talk about pulling the place down: two pools did close to be replaced by Clissold Leisure Centre, which may be slathered in fashionable architectural mores but doesn't make you feel anything at all. Clissold was mired in financial controversy when it first opened in 2002 (then shut, then opened again): overpriced, oversized and over in one of London's poorest boroughs. It all looks very modern: a giant glass box with masses of formed concrete shapes, smooth lines, open views and light, everywhere light. The changing areas are efficient and spacious (though there's a finickety no-shoes rule, like the kind of anxious afterthought of people with white carpets). The pool area is clean, clear, minimal; Japanese screen-style cupboards to decrease clutter, a massive high ceiling with slices lifted and glassed like webbed fingers. The 25m pool itself is two metres deep throughout and deck-edged, so clearly intended for fast and serious swimming, an intention backed up by the intimidating size of the timing display at one end. There is a strange anomaly – a low screen divides this pool from the baby one, which would have been better configured elsewhere on the floor plan. You can almost hear the architects crying at the sight of a giant plastic red toadstool in the corner, completely ruining the clarity of their low-colour vision.

This is not old versus new; not modern-phobic. It's fantastic to swim in a clean, light facility like Clissold. But our sturdy old stock has much to commend it, too. And it would be dreadful if we lost sight of that in our rush to the future.

After a bumpy start, this architectural new-comer has settled in well.

King's Hall Leisure Centre

Address 39 Lower Clapton Road, Hackney, London E5 0NU
Phone 0208 985 2158
Web www.better.org.uk/leisure/king-s-hall-leisure-centre

Clissold Leisure Centre

Address 63 Clissold Road, Hackney, London N16 9EX
Phone 0207 254 5574
Web www.better.org.uk/leisure/clissold-leisure-centre

CRYSTAL PALACE POOL

If swimming is your church, then Crystal Palace Pool is your Westminster Abbey, the full smells and bells, high altar experience. Architecturally it's closer to a modern cathedral, a Liverpool or Coventry, and in time the London Aquatic Centre could lure the congregation away, but for now Crystal Palace is the main temple of serious swimming. It's the sort of place where you say you're going 'training', rather than 'for a swim'; the kind of place where PB means personal best, not peanut butter. I recommend finding your most professional-looking costume, and genuflecting on your way in.

For a national centre (the first purpose-built one in the country), it's not the most accessible place, but if you get lost in the park on the way, there's an odd diversion to enjoy: a collection of the first dinosaur statues ever realised. Made in the 1850s by Benjamin Waterhouse Hawkins, they're now almost comical because of their peculiar (if understandable) inaccuracies,

If you like concrete, space and light then this is the pool for you.

having been constructed even pre-*Origin of Species*. The building continues the dinosaur theme with its 1960s concrete skeleton arrayed against the sky like the dirty grey bones of a pterodactyl in flight. This is one of a handful of Grade II listed pools in London, and it displays that heritage via an imposing frontage of glass and concrete, and a vast interior full of 1960s design classics: lots of dark wood, stone textured walls and concrete, again. The newer additions like the entrance systems look flimsy in comparison, a little dwarfed in the space. That's also how mere mortals may feel as they tread in the footsteps of the many magnificent sportspeople who've trained here.

There's room for a good party in the changing rooms, but there the fun stops. Poolside, the atmosphere is intense. There are two enormous glass walls, red plastic spectator seating down one side, and banks of daunting timing paraphernalia. The pool is one of the few 50m ones in the capital, is the same depth all along, and the water is a degree or two cooler than most public pools, at training temperature. There are no grab rails at either end, just a tiny ledge to momentarily balance on; if a swimmer

has stopped, it's likely that they're timing lengths rather than fancy a chat. It's not deck-edged (where the water is level with the edge), so some people rate it as a 'slow' pool, though maybe they are just the bad losers. Yes, it is the kind of place where people talk about fast and slow pools, but if too much serious athleticism is intimidating, there is always a head-up breaststroker in the slow lane, this also being the only pool for local residents.

If the possibility of being in the company of greatness doesn't spur you on, maybe the thought that you're being watched through the circular underwater observation windows, like a specimen in a zoo, will. Beyond the main pool is the diving area, whose iconic triple diving platforms look like more pieces of a dinosaur skeleton, maybe the scapula. It's an added pleasure to lift your head as you swim and watch young divers, maybe our next Olympic hopefuls, plunging with great style from the top board.

One of the three Grade II listed buildings, along with Marshall Street and the RAC Club.

Crystal Palace National Sports Centre

Address Ledrington Road, London SE19 2BB
Phone 0208 778 0131
Web www.better.org.uk/leisure/crystal-palace-national-sports-centre

CAMBERWELL LEISURE CENTRE AND DULWICH LEISURE CENTRE

Were these pools not just a mile or so apart and of similar provenance, they would definitely each merit a separate entry. As it is, it seems appropriate that they have to share, as they have so much in common already – from fixtures and fittings to chunks of their histories. Both were designed by the same architects, Spalding and Cross, and opened in 1892 within months of each other. Both are run now by the same company who seem to have bulk-bought their interiors; both have cafés, with the same colour chairs, in their reception areas; both have small serviceable changing rooms decked out with the same tiles and dark mock-wood lockers. Each has a 25m pool in that thickly glazed brick-shape tiling, interior high ceilings with inverted V's of glass in their roofs beyond a network of restored ducts and struts and pipes; where each used to have two main pools in their 'Baths' days, they now only have one. Both are brightly lit but not garishly over-signed; both have charm in equal measure, and as a result are equally in demand. They are excellent examples of how to renovate: what to keep and what to throw away. You see why it's impossible to choose between them.

Camberwell Leisure Centre has an impressive red-brick frontage with its old name, Camberwell Public Baths, written in ornate gold letters high up on the Flemish edifice; it still uses the original entrance with its traditional browny-cream patterned Victorian tiling. The substantial corridor down to the pool has modern sloping skylights and there's a large, wooden, half-glassed door through which you get your first glimpse of the water. They've divided the original pool into two with a boom to provide a swimming area

On the edge of Peckham, a really well-used and well-loved restored pool.

and a small teaching pool, which means that the shallow end is already deep – not a pool for playtime for anyone under about five-foot-six. The pool is retiled, so the modern end-guttering feels sleek. Here, the restored spectator balcony is picked out in a delicate blue, and there are large decorative circles cut out of the roof struts.

At Dulwich, while the original frontage still exists (still with the sign Dulwich Public Baths up top, the same as at Camberwell) there is a brand-new entrance on a side road, Crystal Palace Road, covered with fashionably rusted metal slats; the reception area has one wall of 'feature wallpaper', a large-pattern print more suited to a smart home in a magazine. At one end of this pool are a few charming white wooden cubicles that would have been changing provision in the original building. The key words are sweet – just the right side of twee, perhaps – and safe, because there's no deep end. It means that this pool is well used by families with small children, and you may even get to join in an encouraging singsong. The whole thing is almost too cute.

Swimming in these places is a similarly warm experience and it may be that local residents would prefer a contrast. At a push, Camberwell has the added advantage of depth throughout, which makes it feel less like a paddle. But both of them offer times for laned adult swimming.

Fortunate to have maintained some of the original pool-side cubicals, it's ideal for the family swim.

Dulwich Leisure Centre

Address 2B Crystal Palace Road, Dulwich, London SE22 9HB
Phone 0844 893 3888
Web www.fusion-lifestyle.com

Camberwell Leisure Centre

Address Artichoke Place, London SE5 8TS
Phone 0207 703 3024
Web www.fusion-lifestyle.com

CHARLTON LIDO

This lido was a refurbishment-in-progress when I swam here, so until it is completely finished, a little imagination is required to see beyond the portaloos, temporary changing areas and builders' hoardings to the new changing area, gym and café. And, while the surroundings feel a little ad hoc, the pool is open for business. The most pleasing aspect of this is the commitment it demonstrates to swimming outdoors in Charlton, against the national tide of closures and underfunding. This is definitely southeast London's gain.

There's not much to commend the immediate surrounds, and from the exterior you could mistake this for a young offender institution or a bleak 1970s holiday park were it not for the cheery 'we are open' banners. You can find echoes of London lidos in each other; this has typical 1930s features such as you'll find at Brockwell and Parliament Hill. Like them, it is a long, low, red-brick slab with rounded curves, small rotundas and metal-framed windows. It is still mostly utilitarian-looking, adorned only with brick portholes high up in the walls, and a

lot of that very particular lido-blue paint. It was unusual in that it had one of the first dedicated children's pools, and instead of the wedding-cake fountain such as at Tooting and Uxbridge lidos it has two cascades, one tucked in each corner by the entrance, that serve as part of the water filtration system. Those features still exist – the children's pool is the first one you see as you come in. The original pool, opened four months before World War Two broke out, was unheated, which suited the ethos of 'the bracing outdoors', and was (handily) more affordable.

The main pool remains as it was: a lovely 50m-long stretch of water, going from very shallow to a depth of 3m, which is deep enough for diving. It feels spacious, generously laned and – the most notable change – warm. The last few years have seen heating added to the pool, but the aim is to keep it at a swimming-friendly 25 degrees. This may be a thank-you nod to the community whose endeavours have kept the place open in lean years; or perhaps cold water is a little too specialised, and the ice-breakers are already well served by the lidos at Tooting

Charlton Lido is a welcome addition for outdoor swimmers.

and Brockwell. And while it's only been open during summer seasons in the past, that too is set to change when it becomes year-round. It'll be a great spot for south Londoners keen to stay outdoors, but less keen to freeze while they're doing it.

The pool is deck-edged, the rougher paving slabs giving onto a softer, almost bouncy surface around the perimeter; there's enough room (just) to create sunbathing areas at either end, helped by those enclosing walls acting as windbreaks. Within the walls, on a good day this is practically a summer holiday in a pool. When there are no clouds and schools are out . . . be prepared to queue.

New commitment to an old pool has meant the installation of a café, a gym and new changing facilities.

Charlton Lido

Address
Hornfair Park, Shooters Hill Road, London SE18 4LX
Phone
0208 856 7389
Web
www.better.org.uk

TOOTING BEC LIDO

Full disclosure: I swim here all year round, through sun and snow, fog and rain; I'm least likely to be here on that blazing summer day when you have to pick your way delicately across the bodies slabbed out on the poolside paving, because I know how it feels to swim here alone.

This book features London's finest – but Tooting Bec Lido tops the lot, not least in size. Its 91m length makes it the largest lido in the UK, beating Jesus Green in Cambridge by dint of being over twice as wide – 33m to their 15m. That width is longer than the length of a standard 25m public pool. Open to the public from mid-May until the end of September, it runs a thriving winter membership scheme the rest of the year. There's only one other unheated London lido – Parliament Hill – open all through the year to the public.

The lido started life as Tooting Bathing Lake in 1906, when digging this massive million-gallon hole was seen as a fine way of occupying local unemployed men. Men built it, they got to play in it – women were grudgingly allowed in for one day a week only. It officially became a lido in the 1930s, when it acquired 'facilities': a filtration system, a tiered-cake fountain and doors on the cubicles so mixed bathing could commence. Those cubicles are now one of the most iconic images of the place, rows of wooden hutches with corrugated roofs down each narrow pool side, their doors painted red, blue, yellow and green. In the 1990s, a new entrance was built at the shallow end, in Art-Deco style (although the pool predates

The largest Lido in Europe, all 91 by 33 metres of unheated water, Tooting is host to the cold water Swimming Championships.

Little has changed here for 100 years, except for the swimwear.

the period by some thirty years). Two changing/shower roundels were also added, made of concrete and steel, which can be pretty unforgiving materials even in summer. A toddlers' pool was built on the grassed area, which on summer days disappears under a sea of blankets and picnics and buggies and sunbathers. There's a wooden sauna cabin in one corner where most winter swimmers huddle gratefully (there is a hard core for whom a sauna is unnecessary cosseting). There are plans now to adapt the original 1906 entrance, still used in winter, into a modern facility for members and lifeguards.

Whichever entrance you use, whichever bit of detailing you admire or not, the pool itself remains as it always has: an enormous blue slab in the heart of Tooting Common. Shielded by trees all round, it feels incredibly protected yet gloriously open. It's possible to entirely forget where you are – 20 minutes from central London; even the noise of the racing trains barely disrupts. It can feel daunting even to the regular swimmer, checking the temperature, wondering: can I make it to the deep end before my fingers freeze? It's a sight for sore eyes, a salve and a sanctuary. Were it not for the fact it would make it too crowded, swimming here should be compulsory.

Tooting Bec Lido

Address
Tooting Bec Road,
Tooting, London
SW16 1RU
Phone
0208 871 7198
Web
www.dcleisurecentres.
co.uk

BROCKWELL LIDO

Aka Brixton Beach, for good reason on a hot day. Or a wet one, even – beaches are rarely packed in the rain, though it can be absolutely delicious and delightful swimming in a downpour. Less so in hail, though, which can feel like aggressive acupuncture from an overenthusiastic practitioner.

The lido sits at the bottom of a long sweep of Brockwell Park, in itself worth a short bus ride or hearty stroll from Brixton town centre. It has all the hallmarks you'd expect of a Grade II listed lido built in the 1930s – a low-slung red-brick building, with any remaining original decoration, the signage and clocks for instance, having an Art-Deco feel: simple geometry, angular functionality. The building, which includes a members' gym, encloses the pool on three sides; the fourth wall has a café set in it – a very good modern British café at that, and *Time Out* award-winning – which you can access separately. An exit turnstile allows you to glimpse how busy it is inside before you pay your money. And while

Brixton Beach - don't expect it to be as quiet as this on a summer's day.

there is only one kind of swimming experience here – cold – there are two kinds of changing experience on offer. For the ordinary punter: a warm room, a small communal shower with modern fixtures, toilets that barely protect your modesty with their thin mock-plywood door, and outdoor lockers that are so tricky to cram your bag into it's like giving birth in reverse. For members, a rather more salubrious affair: large indoor lockers, fat benches, and a tad more privacy for your ablutions.

Because it squats in the middle of this low building in a park, the 50m pool feels protected while offering armfuls of sky. Previously, it's only been open seasonally (May-ish to October-ish), but in 2012 a group successfully lobbied for some winter swimming action, which can be accessed on a swim-by-swim basis, unlike nearby Tooting Lido which is open to members only from October to May. It's hard not to draw other comparisons between this pool and Tooting Lido because of their proximity. This one is laned, so feels much more controlled. It's smaller and shallower too, so is often a degree warmer and when the temperatures are inching too slowly up or too quickly down, one degree can make quite a difference. The shallows here are very shallow (knees-scraping-on-the-bottom shallow) and there's a ledge just below the surface at the deep end, so turns can be problematic. It's also deemed

Shallow and long, Brockwell has everything for serious swimmers and families alike.

to be a 'slow' pool, and if you're swimming in the lane next to the edge you can certainly feel that – the drop between pool edge and water gives it a certain choppiness.

One thing the two pools share is a sense of community; they both have committed groups of swimmers who will be in the water on good days and bad. These are the people who campaign for places surviving and improving; to those groups, in whatever pool, campaigning on behalf of all of us: thank you.

Brockwell Lido

Address Brockwell Park, Dulwich Road, London SE24 0PA
Phone 0207 274 3088
Web www.fusion-lifestyle.com/centres/Brockwell_Lido

HAMPTON POOL

Another pool another campaign history, this time revolving around a local council's desire to close it and a group of committed swimmers deciding to take it over and run it themselves, people willing to put themselves out for the greater swimming good. Their reward is not selfish, shared as it is with thousands of other people – this is a very busy and successful pool.

Why so busy and successful? Two obvious reasons: it's outdoors, and it's heated. We love an outdoor pool, don't we, despite – or perhaps because of – our climate. Maybe such pools speak to some part of our cold, repressed selves, fed up with being battered down by chilly north winds, and maybe these places satisfy, however fleetingly, a need to feel just a little bit free under our own terms. And of course the 'heated' part of the equation makes that 'free' sensation a bit more reasonable – we may be primal warriors, but we're sensible primal warriors.

And Hampton Pool is certainly heated. Even on a mild day it's a positively tropical 28 degrees, which means there's steam coming off the pool. One might conclude that this is too hot to be a serious swimmers' pool, but the number of plastic bottles and waterproofed training schedules at the shallow end at any given time of the day shows that's not true. It's also 36m long, which means you can brush up on your maths (how many lengths makes a mile?*) while you enjoy your swim.

First, though, there's the car park to negotiate, so pot-holed it's practically Derbyshire. The changing facilities are smart enough, bright and primary-coloured, but be careful: there's a frosted-glass door between the changing bit and the loos and if you're going to scamper around naked twixt the

An exceptionally popular pool for families and serious swimmers alike.

two, that door is sometimes left open. As well as the main pool there's a small children's pool, and both are set into a flat field that looks like the back garden of a semi-rural pub, with plastic chairs and white-painted brick outbuildings. There used to be a diving board at one end but it hasn't survived; the only 'fun' way to get in is via an old slide (not recommended for anyone over 12 stone). There are usually two or three swimming lanes taking up half the pool, with the other half free-form, though as the lanes are quite narrow, making overtaking a very conscious choice. But that's balanced by the warm fatigue at the end of a session, from the extra energy exerted by frequently overtaking people.

One of the pleasures of a good swim is the coffee afterwards, and there's plenty of space on the roof terrace to sit and drink one, eat a bowl of porridge maybe, and watch and learn from other swimmers.

* The answer is: 45 lengths is just over a mile.

Open 365 days of the year, after your swim you can sit in the gallery cafe commentating on the other swimmers.

Hampton Pool

Address High Street, Hampton, Middlesex TW12 2ST
Phone 0208 255 1116
Web www.hamptonpool.co.uk

HILLINGDON LIDO

Through a narrow brick archway is a fountain, created in a tiered style that will be familiar to anyone, like this writer, who is a fan of 1930s-built lidos. To the left of the fountain, a sweep of paving leads up to a rather elegant white cruise-ship-like building. And just behind it, a beautiful 67m outdoor pool, made glorious by judicious surrounding design and, of course, by being open to the skies.

The centre's full name is Hillingdon Sports and Leisure Complex, which tells you that this isn't just a lido. The indoor pool is that rare treasure, 50m in length, but what the complex gives with one hand, it takes with the other – that 50m is often parcelled up into tiny squares, so if you

While the pool itself is old, it has been well refurbished and is rapidly becoming an established part of the outdoor swimming scene.

If you want to swim the full 50 metres indoors, it is worth checking the busy class timetable first.

outdoor cubicles and a shower building – all the showers are open to the gaze (the toilets, thank goodness, are hidden round the back). Everything is long, low and stylish. Central to it all is the 67m-long pool – described officially as the shape of a '12-sided star', but in reality they look more like ears on each side of a head. It's a crisp cold swim, underlined by the whiteness of the tile and the sharpness of the black lines on the bottom of the pool. The pool itself is unlaned, so a little inner discipline is required, but frankly, if you're getting in a cold pool on most days of the English summer, that's probably one thing you're not short of.

There's nothing high round the perimeter of the pool, so you never feel cramped in and it's a chance to drop your guard and lift your gaze. Beyond the main pool is a small (heated) splash pool for children. But brace yourself when you're showering: they are not only public, but also cold. That's a cruel touch, maybe one that only the absolute purists appreciate.

seek a swim uninterrupted by ropes, booms and other people swimming in random zigzags, check the timetable. Housed in a large, white, professional-looking hangar, it's smart and uncluttered. On one side is a swoosh-shaped 'fun' pool, that particular inner circle of hell beloved by children and slumped in by desperate parents who could happily curl up and sleep in this over-warm puddle if squabbling toddlers would just keep the noise down.

However, through a separate turnstile: the lido.

The whole area was recently refurbished, and it's beautiful. Chic and understated, white, greys, even the light-pink slabs round the pool work the same colour palette. To one side a curve of

Hillingdon Sports and Leisure Complex

Address Gatting Way, Uxbridge, Middlesex UB8 1ES
Phone 0845 130 7324
Web www.fusion-lifestyle.com

PUTNEY LEISURE CENTRE

There is bound to be at least one pool in London that will pull your memory strings, whether or not you grew up here. Putney Leisure Centre does that for me. I grew up in Sutton Coldfield, a middle-class suburb of Birmingham; Wyndley Leisure Centre was my local pool. Putney opened in 1968 and Wyndley in 1970, so it's no surprise how much design these two public pools share, along with the glass, the sparkly concrete floor and untempered shapes. But Putney is not included on this list purely out of personal nostalgia. It has great architectural merit, and real modern heritage.

The building is a shiny white block on a slope, so set on stilts at the front. There are separate men's and ladies' changing rooms, which have shower cubicles, but the largest area is reserved for the 'changing village', the communal changing area, with open showers and free-range children. Here, as with most changing villages, the ceilings are low and the warren-like layout is dark and confusing, but that only serves to increase the sense of light that hits you as you enter the pool area.

The pool is quite an eye-opener: bright and clean, maximum light with minimum fuss. There are huge windows everywhere, which form entire walls. There are thin, glazed strip windows as well as triangular ones that almost seem to hold up the ceiling so it becomes a series of floating V's. To one side, screened by jungle plants, is an 1980s Jacuzzi pool with a glassed-in fitness block above it. There's nothing mean or boxy about any of this design; it feels generous and (though most of it is, gulp, over 40 years old) contemporary. This is helped by the way they've kept what works – the stylish galleried seating is the original dark wood rather than garish ranks

Another pool where it is worth checking the timetable for if you want to swim the full 33 metres.

of bright plastic. There's even a little home-made charm – a wooden shelf arrangement for storing your bag.

The pool itself is an L-shape, the short leg being a diving area, and was one of the first pools built with the diving area incorporated into the pool, rather than the more expensive option of having two separate areas. And this is one of the few places where the diving boards remain intact and in use. The long leg gives a 33m swim, but the pool is often split into two, with swimmers given lanes across the diving bay. That's not the best way to enjoy this pool – it's deep (obviously), shorter (obviously) and there's no grab rail at the board end. But there's a timetable, so you can avoid that.

Even if this doesn't bring you nostalgia, it will offer you some modern classic design. And, of course, a swim.

Fortunate to have retained their original diving boards, this is one of the first pools to have had a diving area incorporated into the pool.

Putney Leisure Centre

Address
Dryburgh Road, Putney, London SW15 1BL
Phone
0208 785 0388
Web
www.dcleisurecentres.co.uk/centres/putney-leisure-centre

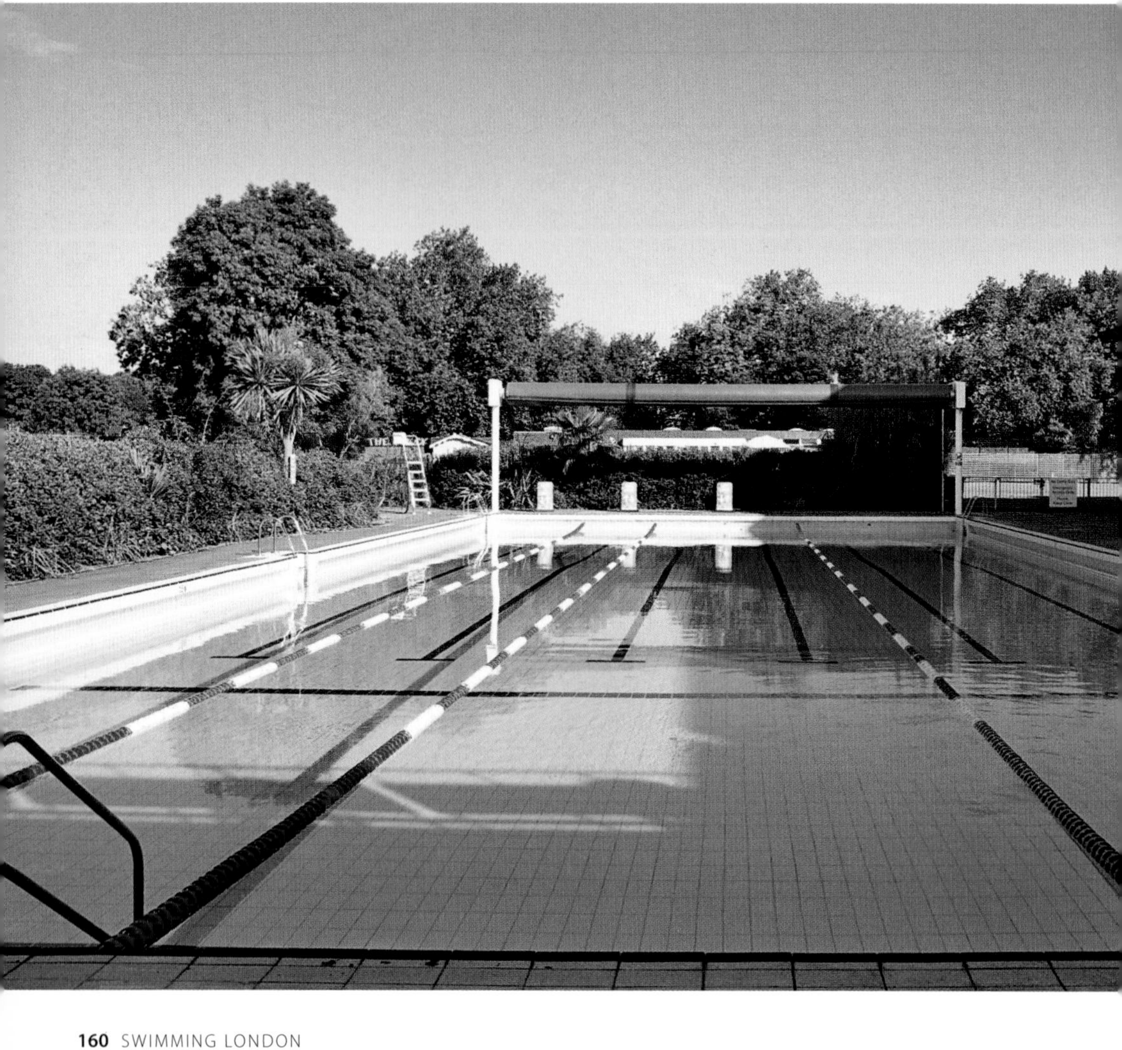

RICHMOND POOLS ON THE PARK

If you are a keen student of hi-tech artefacts, this is the pool to visit. In the changing village is a strange machine, a bright-orange plastic booth that looks like it was designed for a *Doctor Who* set in the 1970s by someone who imagined the future, and then went a little bit further and decided that towels would be obsolete. Yes, it's a drying booth, the only one I've ever seen, though as I've never seen it working, it may be a prototype. But the pointlessness of it, the attempt to mechanise (and probably monetise) the perfectly simple task of drying oneself, is an amusing idea.

Drying booths aside, the people of Richmond are very lucky. Steeped in royal history, and with the finest open land in London, Richmond is what people mean when they say 'leafy borough'. The pool complex is in what's left of Old Deer Park, which is now mostly used for golf and rugby. Surrounded by trees, this two-storey brick building offers two main pools as well as a gym .

The outdoor pool is accessed via plastic strips redolent of the entrance to a butcher's fridge. There are areas for lawn-lounging and the lido is sheltered by hedging and dotted with tall cordylines, so we could be in a south coast town. Deep enough to dive at one end, there are shallow slippery steps at the other, which give a gentle entry but spoil the possibility of a fluid swim – every time you return to this end, there's nothing to push off, so you find yourself crawling halfway up the steps like a creature evolving. It is, though, a lovely 33m, and heated, which seems counter-intuitive given that it is

Only open in the summer, this is a popular heated outdoor pool in a leafy borough of London.

only open in the summer. You can, though, still feel the cold air on any body part sticking up out of the water.

The pool has the politest lane dividers: you can choose 'nice and easy' or 'fast crawl'. The view is of sky and trees, and for that alone it's worth a few lengths of backstroke, though you'll hit your head on the steps if not fully vigilant.

On the other side of a plate-glass window is the indoor pool, which is also 33m long and clean and hot. The interior décor – the tiny mosaic tiles or square white ones, the huge windows – give it a similar sense of space to Putney Leisure Centre. There are plenty of communal showers, but nothing private, this being a village. As you towel yourself dry, that prehistoric, time-consuming process, you can look over at the drying booth and dream of the future.

As well as a teaching pool, there's an additional indoor pool that is open all year round.

Old Deer Park

Address
Twickenham Road,
Richmond, Surrey
TW9 2SF

Phone
0208 940 0561

Web
www.springhealth.net
/richmond/index.html

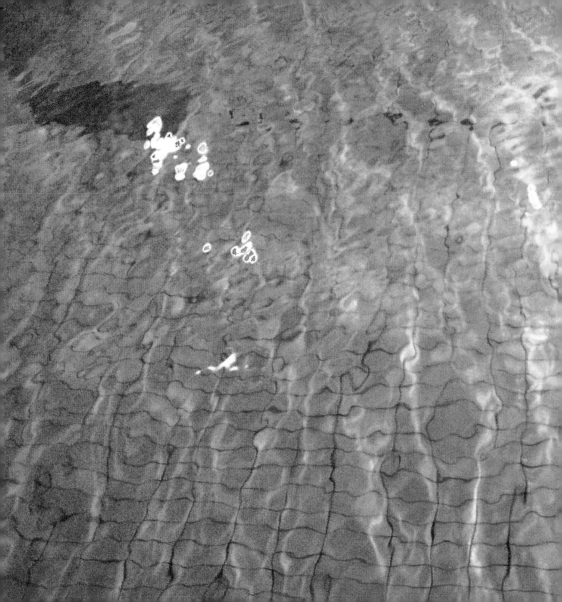

DENHAM LAKE

Officially this book features pools within London and a boundary map shows the lake right on the cusp of South Bucks, which is almost definitely not London; you could throw a stick from it and hit the M25. But this open-water treat is too good to exclude for reasons of geography.

This is a privately owned site, a water-ski club, and while swimming and water-skiing don't generally make a happy marriage, they've made this one work by restricting swimming times to a couple of evenings and one early morning per week. There's also no swimming when the water is below 12 degrees, which generally chimes with the open-water training season. Let that be a clue as to the clientele: there are a lot of wetsuited people here doing serious laps then timing themselves stripping down. An added bonus: if you've never seen anyone try to get out of a wetsuit at speed, it has a certain comedy value.

You don't have to be an athlete to swim here, but it's not really for the chatty dawdler. The atmosphere is friendly but intense, even though driving through villages and then down a bumpy country lane to get here might remind you of craning for that first glimpse of a rented holiday cottage. The wooden chalet-style clubhouse perpetuates that feeling – and so does the view. It's a 20-acre lake enclosed and protected by trees and reeds, a great whack of sky and an air of peaceful seclusion. Twenty acres is a great size: not so small you can take it all in in one snap, but not so big it's daunting. There's an established system of signing in and form filling: a straightforward tick list of disclaimers, then once you've paid and got your wristband, you can go and change. Wetsuits aren't obligatory but a bright

Up the road from the Uxbridge Lido, you can do two outdoor swims in one day.

swim cap is – bring one with you so you can be easily spotted against the dark water.

The facilities are Brownie camp basic. One small wooden cupboard, one loo, one shower, a soggy floor. Getting in and out of the water is similarly basic: you either jump or dive in and then haul yourself out on rickety steps clinging to a piece of drainpipe. But none of that matters. The water is a thick olive green but feels soft and tastes lakey. There's a set of coloured buoys marking out the route, and one circuit can either be 750m or 1km depending which colour you follow. It couldn't be simpler. Careful sighting helps you round the

course, watched scornfully by some resident swans. Even when busy it has that focused and meditative atmosphere, and whether you're in training or lost in your own thoughts, you feel part of something special. Spend an hour with (if you're lucky) an early or late sun on your back, and afterwards dry out on deck and enjoy watching an L-plated water-skier coming a cropper.

While the facilities are basic, the water is idyllic.

Denham Waterski Club

Address North Orbital Rd, Denham, Bucks UB9 5HE
Phone 01895 820007
Web www.denhamwaterski.com

HAM LAKE

We're in Ham. Its name derives from the olde English word Hamme, meaning 'place in the bend of the river', and that's where it is, a river bend south of Richmond. Ham Lake is artificial, formed from old gravel pits, and connected to the Thames via a lock. The lake is used for young mariners learning to sail, so swim times are restricted and run by a sports company during the summer months. It costs no more than entry to a public pool, and there are coached or 'just swim' sessions on their calendar. A visit here requires an early start, but there are substantial benefits.

I arrive before sun-up one mid-September morning. Across the parking field is a garage door painted with a dragon mural – more karate dojo than serene swimming spot. To the left, a functional block of low buildings, beyond them a stack of kayaks; to the right, a couple of people warming their hands on thermos cups, and, as I get nearer, the lake itself huddling in a hollow (the pit of its origins). Against the dark morning it looks chilly and flat black, but not daunting in size. Small boats bob in groups; a flock of Canada geese take off from the water and flap away with a muscular beat. I change in what reminds me of an old school changing room – a bit beaten-up but clean and functional and warmer inside than out, at this time of day, this time of year. As I pad down the entry slope to the water, the skies have lightened. There's a 600m route round the perimeter marked out by white buoys; I strike out for the first one. Where the water is fed from the Thames it feels silty, with a layer of chill on the top. Further away

A very peaceful setting- Ham Lake is certainly worth getting up early for.

from the inlet opening, towards the far reach of the lake and still shaded by the hedging on the bank, the water is more crisply dark and silky; the first fallen leaves of the season dance in small unknown patterns on the surface.

Then, the sun comes up. With an almost audible pop the first arc of gold appears above the tips of the low hedging where it hits leaves and they bask in the warm glow. The small boats reveal their bright blue; white plane trails crisscross the sky. I go once round. And again, until my fingers and toes complain about the temperature. Reluctantly – it's always hard to leave a swim when the sun is up, even when it's not yet a warm sun – I wade back up the slope and indulge in a pleasingly warm shower.

I sit on a bench overlooking the lake and have coffee from a flask and a banana. There are two other swimmers in now, and I watch them. The sun is luck, the rest is mostly nature, and some design and it's a great way to start the day.

The view from a bench after a swim is almost enough to make you get back in again.

Thames Young Mariners

Address Ham Fields, Richmond TW10 7RX
Phone 07834 483 989
Web www.rgactive.com

PORCHESTER BATHS

There is something about Porchester Baths that is a reminder of council chambers from the 1930s. The entrance hall, with its heavy wood doors and polished brass handles, marble and stained glass, is where one might imagine office clerks in tatty suits and wire-frame glasses spilling sheaths of hand-written documents from battered leather briefcases as they scurry between important meetings. Which is appropriate, as swimming is, of course, an extremely important business.

Built in 1925, the exterior has a pillared grandeur that would be best appreciated from a distance, if that were possible. Inside, the modern reception paraphernalia has been tastefully incorporated into the fabric; although the changing rooms are serviceable enough, beyond them the baths have seen better days. The pools are definitely shabby, but it's the kind of shabby – a cracked bottom, mouldy grouting, chalky water and steps so worn down you can see the historic raw concrete underneath – that's very familiar in pools of this age, making it comfortable, undemanding, homely even. But it would need more than a 'homely feel' to make the swim worth it.

It has more. Despite its interwar construction, this is a 30m pool in those generous Victorian proportions that are echoed in the splendid layout of the room – there's a high gilded spectators' balcony and one huge almost-blank church-like wall. The light from the circular windows along the upper walls ripples on the water; on a good day you can swim blissfully in and out of the punctuating sunspots.

There's also a long skylight the length of the domed ceiling. But this pool is a haven of

dark intensity compared to the barn next door: a strut-roofed annexe with a teaching pool, painted so clean-bright you're going to need shaded goggles. Sharp needles of light from one spills across to the other and they're both very well-used pools, but the lanes in the main pool are generous and the water cool enough for a decent swim. The tiles were once white, there are red lines scratched on the bottom and satisfyingly rounded guttering at each end.

You can come here just to swim. However, five years after the pool opened, what is now the oldest spa in London was added, and swimming is available as part of a spa package. This spa is dimly lit with green plastic recliners and faded fake plants under hammered bronze ceilings. When you make your way down an ornate stairwell past a tiny plunge pool to the bowels of the building you end up in corridors of tiles crackle-glazed and puffed-up like fat biscuits, a labyrinth of pipes and doors that lead to hot rooms and Turkish or Russian baths. Further down there are steam rooms, saunas and large marble slabs for a bit of healthy pummelling. The spa offers separate men's, women's and couples' times; this is not the fluffy white gowns and gentle wafting of the modern spa, but a half-day here can be whiled away in an unfancy kind of accessible peace.

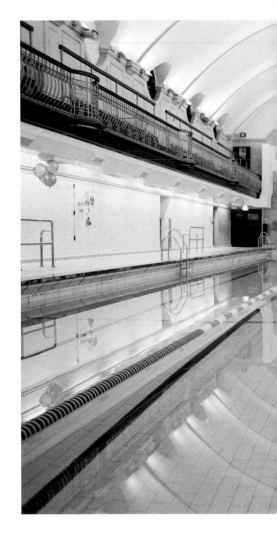

With a high gilded spectator's balcony, with almost church-like features, this is a place to come and swim in silence.

Porchester Baths

Address
Queensway, Bayswater, London W2 5HS
Phone
0207 792 2919
Web
www.better.org.uk

HERON LAKE AND THORPE LAKE

The act of moving through water remains roughly the same whether you're wild swimming, open-water swimming or just plain swimming. But open-water swimming is on the rise and if that means that the lakes edging London become more accessible, then who cares what it's called.

Both Heron and Thorpe Lakes are situated almost on top of the M25 – at Heron, when you're on the home stretch of the 1km swim route, breathe to the left and you'll see the blue motorway boards above the shield of trees. Stop for a second and you'll hear the not-so-distant traffic. At Thorpe Lake, you may get the added bonus of screeching: the curls and loops of Thorpe Park's rides tower above the treeline. But trees do buffer a lot of the noise and you can pull your focus close and concentrate on lovely open swims.

Wetsuits are not obligatory at Thorpe Lake, but they are at Heron Lake unless you're training for the Channel (or similar). At both, slick matt-black bodies almost glide atop the water, while on land people struggle in and out of their tight casings. Open water might suggest freedom, but the actuality is often clad in neoprene – exactly the opposite.

At Heron, entry to the lake is via a jetty, where advice and conversation flow generously. Then you have to make your way down a slope, like a slanted green-baize snooker table, and step into the waters. There is nothing to be gained here by faffing around – just set off round the corner for the first of the huge inflatable yellow pyramids that mark your way.

The portfolio of open water swimming spots is growing rapidly, and Heron Lake is one of the latest additions.

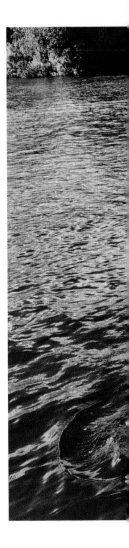

Each one says 'Turn here' in large letters; ignore that and you'll end up in the hedgerow, so it's good advice. There are two routes here – once round is 1km, while there's a shorter 400m route if you're less optimistic. The water is green and feels clean, though visibility is minimal – if you're following feet, they'll disappear barely a metre in front of you. On a couple of the stretches there are visible underwater ropes attached to various buoys; on the long length right across the lake, there's little to sight apart from the yellow pyramid buoy way in the distance.

Up the road at Thorpe Lake (which, if I had to state a preference, would get the nod), you cross a pontoon to get to the facilities. Head for the London bus which serves as swimming office. Here you'll sign in, pay and get your wristband so they can count you in and out, which is standard practice. Advice on the day's water conditions is also available.

There are three options here: 400m, 750m or 1.5km. The run to the first buoy is short and a good opportunity to catch your breath before you set off across the water. If you're doing the 1.5km you

can't see the end of the lake from the bus, so will have a kayaker keeping a close eye on you. It's very clean, with great visibility. And yes, the advice was right. It was choppy on the return.

Just over the hedge you'll see all the rollercoasters, and maybe hear the screams from nearby Thorpe Park.

Thorpe Water Ski Lake

Address Thorpe Road, Chertsey, Surrey KT16 8PH
Phone 07770 391966
Web www.nowca.org/lake/9/Thorpe-Swimming-Lakes-%28NOWCA-HQ%29

Heron Lake

Address The Tony Edge National Centre, Hythe End, Wraysbury, Middlesex TW19 6HW
Phone 07780 994772
Web www.openwaterswimminguk.co.uk

FERRIS MEADOW LAKE

You know that feeling when you have to get up at some unearthly time, and you imagine you'll be the only one in the world awake? It feels like a magical hour, a quality of light (or dark) you never normally see. Then you step outside and discover the roads busy with people going about their business: 'Wow, I had no idea all this went on while I lay sleeping.' You'll get a similar feeling driving up the bumpy country lane to Ferris Meadow Lake: the sensation that there's nothing and no one around, that you're about to arrive at some deserted spot and be a lone, brave swimmer constantly checking over your wetsuited shoulder. Then, suddenly, a field that serves as a car park will open up in front of you and you'll see that you are not alone.

Parking in a field has a slight festival or car boot sale feel to it, until you see that there's a lot of people around fully clad in rubber (wetsuits are not obligatory, but many here are training for open-water events where they are). Once you've signed in at an open-sided wooden cabin, the changing area (for women, at least) is a small room under some stairs in a more substantial building. It's not sophisticated. Nor is it supposed to be.

The reason for coming here is the lake itself. A huge circle of water with a small beach entry, surrounded by mixed trees and reeds, with some breaks for emergency exits. There are buoys marking 750m and 400m round the circle, but if it's your first trip, a lifeguard will ask you to head for the nearest

The facilities are rustic but you come here for the water and the course here is worth travelling for.

buoy, to check that you can actually swim. The entry beach is busy with people starting and finishing, peeling rubber on and off, but it's a different feeling once you get past that first buoy. It's peace. The water feels textured and dark – you won't see your own hand, let alone other swimmers who'll be on top of you before you know it. (A word of warning – don't expect a polite 'I'm so sorry' from anyone who bashes into you; for 'athletes' in training, normal life etiquette goes out the window.) This place prides itself on putting swimming first and sport second, so it doesn't feel like heresy to put your head up and take a few slow strokes while you appreciate the place. The lake is generous, the planting is lush, coots and swans weave in and out of us swimming invaders.

Changing in the cubby hole, with its tiny cramped benches not designed for adults performing difficult costume manoeuvres, will bring you back down to earth. But as you clutch a warm drink outside, enjoy the friendly atmosphere and the view: at the furthest reaches of the lake, the black freestyling arms become giant-spider-like, each stroke producing a silvery splash that glints against the dark water. All you can hear is that repetitive splash, and maybe the distinctive squawk of parakeets, flashing brilliant-green as they swoop overhead.

Don't forget that if you are swimming outdoors, the birds have as much right to be there as you do!

Ferris Meadow Lake

Address Ferry Lane, Shepperton, Middlesex TW17 9LH
Phone 07531 745 133
Web www.sheppertonopenwaterswim.co.uk

THE THAMES

You can't write a book about swimming round London and ignore that a river runs through it. Whichever way you look at the city, the Thames is a historic river that has defined us. Our rights to swim in parts of it have been discussed in the highest chambers of the land. It's busy, tidal and intimidating. It's dangerous in places, and is sometimes described as a health hazard.

But it's also functional and beautiful, a contemplation and a solace, its calming influence spreading beyond its banks. There are informal groups of keen outdoor swimmers who set out to conquer the length of it over weeks and months, right up as far as is legal (which is about 150 miles of it). There's a guide – 'I ♥ the Thames' – where the river is broken into 77 manageable swims, including all the entry and exit points. One swim adventure company offers 'Thames trekking' but they are based towards Oxford, where it's much prettier and safer, and hence outside the remit of this book. Individuals tackle it as a personal challenge (sometimes for TV, sometimes just because it's there). These days it's clean enough for otters – I spotted one once by Battersea Bridge and I swear it winked at me.

I certainly wouldn't advocate getting in without some planning. If you want to understand why it's dangerous to just jump in wherever you please, see what it's like from a boat. What you'll realise, as you peer over the side, is that it's hard to see things in the water until you are right on top of them. And as a swimmer, that's the last place you want a boat to be. So if you do get in the water, as a minimum you need to wear a brightly coloured swim cap to make yourself visible. And you'll need to keep your wits about you – it can be a thrilling but anxious experience.

I have lived in London for longer than I haven't and (as this book bears witness) swum round big chunks of it. But I thought I would never swim in the Thames without guides, kayakers in formation, a marching band, plus a full support team of helicopters, ambulances and a SWAT team of rescue personnel. Then I found some organised swims. They prove that despite the stories of illness and danger, despite the legislation and fears that 'something bad might happen', swimming in the London Thames is eminently possible, and totally enjoyable. One of the swims listed here is only open to members of South London Swimming Club (SLSC), who

are affiliated with Tooting Lido – it's included here for scenic value, but there are others that are public. I found them all online. My final bit of advice is: don't, if you can help it, swallow too much river.

While it is no longer permissable to swim in the river Thames between Crossness and Putney Bridge, there are still organised swims in the more bucolic parts of the river.

HAMPTON COURT TO KINGSTON BRIDGE

This swim takes you from under the watchful gilded gaze of Hampton Court Palace to just before the noble arches of Kingston Bridge. Around a thousand swimmers undertake two and a quarter miles of Thames, where wetsuits are not compulsory but most people wear them regardless. (And of course your time will be faster in a wetsuit, if that is important to you.) This is a one-off swim in mid-summer; the date changes year by year. It isn't classified as a fun swim because of the distance – it tends to attract more hardened 'competitors'; the word 'race' is in the name of the organisers (Human Race) and most people see it as that. That attitude is not obligatory but given the average water temperature, even in the summer, it makes sense not to hang around.

The course is also tidally assisted – some years that can make a huge difference, others less so. The race is organised with a staggered start depending on your speed per kilometre, so you may overtake and get overtaken, but it means it's not too chaotic when it comes to getting in, so don't worry – you're not just thrown in with a thousand other swimmers. And once any crowds at the beginning have thinned out and the speed merchants have thrashed away into the distance, this is an utterly lovely swim.

It's very safe – the daily river traffic is kept well away and guide kayakers line the route to your right – and picturesque; sometimes you're swimming alongside grassy paths, sometimes boats and the gardens of beautiful houses (it's not an efficient way to conduct a Thames-side property search, though). When you swim through the final 'gates', which pick up the timing chip in your hat, you get a real sense of achievement, whatever your final time.

The swim is open to anyone over 18, and you must be able to complete the route in under four hours.

The historic river, now the starting point of one of the busiest public swims.

Swim Info

Web

humanrace.co.uk/
events/open-water-
swimming/hampton-
court-swim/

KINGSTON BRIDGE TO ROYAL CANOE CLUB, TEDDINGTON

This is a low-key swim of just under a mile organised each summer by SLSC, of which I am a member. In the busier Hampton Court swim, there are enough swimmers to form a critical mass. Here, it must be a curious sight for the passer-by as they come around the corner and chance upon a group of people in costumes and swim hats hanging round for the signal to get in and go.

The entry point is on the downstream side of Kingston Bridge, north bank. It's surrounded by new-build flats with frosted-glass balconies and walkways, while an indoor shopping centre is just around the corner. Once you're swimming, though, you quickly leave that urbanity behind and are soon going alongside grass banks – often the ends of huge private gardens. This stretch, too, is tidal and resulted in the quickest mile I've ever swum, ending at the jetty for the local canoe club.

Putting your feet down finally, the sludge of the river comes up through your toes and silts up the water, making a quick exit preferable. This was the first swim that I had ever done in the river and when organisers handed me a standard printed note to give to my doctor, should I fall ill in the following few days, it did give me pause. There are factors that reduce your chances of catching something, including swimming regularly in the Thames, which seems a bit of a Catch 22, and being over 40, about the only time that being 'older' is a bonus. The only way to take part in this particular swim is to join SLSC, which is open to all.

The central part of the river Thames is always busy, so it's always safest to keep to the banks, even in a public swim.

The canoe club, where the swim ends.

Swim Info

Web www.slsc.org.uk

PISSARRO SWIM

This takes you from the Black Lion pub in Hammersmith to Chiswick Pier. There are two options here. First, the 'acclimatisation swims', which happen informally on specific tides; second, the Pissarro Race, which happens once a year (flexible dates, based on optimal neap tides). The race has been running for twelve-plus years – it's a kilometre and a bit, and offers a very different atmosphere from the Great London Swim (see below). The acclimatisation swims are free to enter and at your own risk – and are truly charming (all details can be found under 'Events' on the Pissarro website).

The start point is like going through a magic portal – just seconds away from a three-laned commuter route and you're in a pastoral haven. All of a sudden, the thrum of buses and nose-to-nose cars are replaced by glorious Georgian houses and picturesque cottages that amble down to a mellow water. You easily spot fellow swimmers lingering in various states of undress

The friendliest and most low key of all the Thames races.

by the Black Lion pub, where there are steps down into the river – bags are taken to the other end so you don't have to pad back here in just your costume. This is all run voluntarily, and it has that friendly welcoming sense of the slightly ad hoc. But of course there's nothing amateur about it – each swim is precisely timed to catch the incoming tide and the river flows quickly here, which you discover if you miss the steps at the end and have to swim against it to get back to them.

The swim takes you up past Chiswick Eyot – a small island in the river – and on to the white jetty just under a mile or so upriver. The water feels gentle and accommodating, and on a summer's evening, with the Thames lapping up on soft grass banks, this feels like freedom in the heart of the capital. If you've never swum in the river and would like to but feel intimidated, then make this your first stop. It's friendly, soft, blissful.

Swim Info

Web www.pissarro.co.uk

An odd sight for tourists, happy swimmers emerging from the River Thames.

THE GREAT LONDON SWIM

At the other end of the spectrum is the Great London Swim, part of the Great Swim series which happens across the country, and is the biggest public event in the capital's swim calendar. Set in one of London's East End docks (the year I did it, it transferred at the last minute from Royal Albert Dock to Millwall Dock due to 'water quality issues' which should have been cheery news) the swim isn't exactly in the Thames, but still definitely feels part of it.

It's 'on the other end of the spectrum' because bucolic this is not. Firstly, being set in the eastern extreme of the city means you are surrounded by new-build tower blocks with a very high glass quotient and smart new cafés that serve said towers, alongside ancient working dock companies that kept this part of the world ticking over for hundreds of years. Secondly, nearly three thousand swimmers take part. In addition, wetsuits are compulsory, even though the water temperature may hit the 20s. This means that your times may be quicker than if you were just in a swimming costume, as the buoyancy they provide helps you glide over the water. The course is a mile, the kind of distance that attracts a wider crowd – it doesn't have the same hardcore spirit of the Hampton Court Swim. But for some it's a real challenge – and the beauty is that this feels celebratory no matter your pace or ability.

Swimmers are set off in waves, and you can select according to your travel plans or how early you like to get up. The venue is absolutely heaving; neoprene-clad bodies who have just swum jostle with those yet to get in; the

Very busy, but well-marshalled, the Great London Swim is a good introduction to the swimming race calendar.

atmosphere feels inclusive and bustling. Once you are shuffling towards the edge of the water with your 'wave', feeling like penguins about to plunge off their little bit of ice floe, it's too late for second thoughts and anyway, you can be carried in on the organised whoops and cheers that send you on your way.

The words 'Millwall Dock' may have made you think of old gangster movies, but actually, it's where the Docklands Sailing and Watersports Centre is based, so the water feels like felt but is surprisingly clean. The course is shaped like a backwards R, and swimming down that first long length is where you set your stride, get into the rhythm of sighting if you haven't had to do that in the pool. This is where the initial jostling might happen – when visibility is poor and the field hasn't yet properly opened out, you can find yourself swimming into people accidentally but very easily, and the same happening to you.

You get to the curve around the top of the R and that's when you realise you really are in the heart of things: Canary Wharf looms over the dockside buildings, the stark white and glass absolutely popping against the sky and yellow brick wharfs. The course then takes you alongside new walkways and long old barges, and then, down the final straight to the end, orange triangle buoys that will read the final time from the chip in your ankle bracelet. Then it's out, under the showers, which are just a couple of hosepipes slung over a bracket, and into the massive tents to change with your fellow competitors.

Despite being busy and wetsuited, there is a great pleasure to be had simply in the taking part. It's not exactly the Olympics but you still get a medal at the end.

Unimaginable 30 years ago, the London Docks is now a popular sailing and watersports site.

CHILDREN'S SECTION

So, what about the children?

No indoor pools in this book specifically exclude children, although in some the shallow end is not very shallow, which makes it tricky for smaller ones. Some of the lakes are only for very able older children (16-plus) who would be judged capable on the day by attendants. Hampstead's three ponds (Men's, Women's and Mixed) don't allow children under eight, and under-16s need to be accompanied by an adult and do an on-the-spot swimming test.

In private gyms and clubs children are often only allowed restricted access. In many of London's municipal pools, the kind of neighbourhood 'everyday' places which are the bread and butter of council provision, dedicated teaching (or 'baby') pools sit alongside normal pools. This is true, too, of quite a few of the pools in this book – the list at the end of this chapter details particular provision for children in those places, where it exists. And lidos in summer wouldn't be complete without the screams of happy children doing handstands in the way of serious swimmers. Some of them also have a dedicated 'paddling pool' for toddlers – specific information on children's provision in lidos is in another list at the end.

In one sense, it could be argued that children are well served by London pools. But statistics about how many children cannot swim don't bear witness to that, and cuts and closures can only make these figures worse. However, even if your child is a serious swimmer, sometimes only a flume or slide is what they are after rather than a pool geared to hard physical exercise. Learning how to enjoy being in the water is an important part of childhood and there's no better way to do it than by playing in it with friends.

There isn't a great deal of choice in London if this is the kind of pool you're after, in the main because of financial considerations – they are expensive to build and run. Below are three of the best places for children (and some honourable mentions). They share two qualities: firstly, the possibility of having a decent swim if your children are old enough to be left to enjoy

Flumes, slides or serious swimming - London has it all for kids and grown-ups alike.

themselves without your supervision. Secondly, the surroundings in each are unpretentious, but experience bears out that children either don't notice or don't care about such peripherals. I visited each of these pools with 'children testers'. It didn't occur to them to critique the exterior or building furniture – fun was the key. They decided the order of appearance here – accordingly, the best is saved until last.

BRENTFORD FOUNTAIN LEISURE CENTRE

Out in west London, this is a huge building with little to commend the exterior. The changing area has a massive amount of space but very little room to actually change in. Inside, there are two pools within the same enormous hall. (This is a key consideration – if you ARE leaving your children to have fun alone, it does help if you're at least in the same room so they can easily find you if there's trouble of the 'water went up my nose' kind. That's not always the case.)

At the far side is a very shallow traditional rectangular pool for swimming – its deepest part is only one metre. On the other, taking up the majority of the space, is a freeform 'leisure pool'. You reach the arena via a tunnel that makes you feel like a gladiator entering the arena (without the roar of a crowd). There's a lot of corrugation in this building, big brightly painted ducts run along the ceilings and there's enough artificial light to brighten a football stadium. The leisure pool has a large sloped and slippery beach area, with some round tiled structures on which to seek refuge. There's a deep-water area, which becomes most fun when the wave machine gets going; there are always some huge floats left out, which are big enough to sit on and pretend you're on a boat.

However, what stands at the centre of the room is the star attraction: the flume. A metal staircase winds its way up – and then you get a lovely long drop – not steep, but long – into a Jacuzzi pool at the bottom. It's impossible, if you're sitting watching in the poolside café, not to smile as a child comes zooming down into the receiving pool, an expression of gleeful fear on their face.

Opportunities for fun and games are endless.

Brentford Fountain Leisure Centre

Address 658 Chiswick High Road, Brentford TW8 0HJ
Phone 0845 456 6675
Web www.fusion-lifestyle.com/centres

WATERFRONT LEISURE CENTRE, WOOLWICH

Although part of a standard southeast London leisure centre with gym and court space, this part is called 'Wild & Wet' to distinguish it from a standard pool. Again, it's all one giant space and there really is a lot going on: 'this can satisfy all ages' said one of my testers, aged 12.

To the right, there's a normal 25m infinity pool, with wide laning in place. So far, so ordinary. But then there's also: a plain small pool with a little bridge; a Jacuzzi; a deep area with a wave machine and waterfalls; and a baby area where animals squirt water (not actual animals, your children may be disappointed to hear). There are big balls to play with, and spouting poles they call 'volcanoes'. There's a set of small bumping slides in a row, perfect for racing. And the centrepiece, the best bit, is a huge slide, called the anaconda slide because it ends in a snake's head. You can see it on your way in, the snaking body coming out of the building and going in again. You can easily lose an hour or two in here, which will at least put off the ordeal of facing the changing facilities again for a while.

Of course you will never
see the pool this quiet.

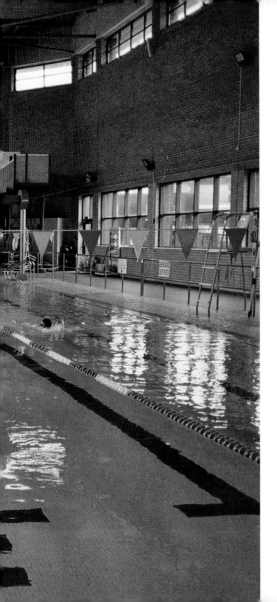

Any swim here comes with the accompaniment of kids screaming and laughing.

Waterfront Leisure Centre

Address Woolwich High Street, Woolwich, London SE18 6DL
Phone 0208 317 5010
Web www.better.org.uk/leisure/waterfront-leisure-centre

WHITE OAK LEISURE CENTRE, SWANLEY

This was the preferred choice both of my testers and myself. It might surprise you – it's not the one with the greatest variety of features. Again, it's a plain exterior that looks like an ageing health centre. Built in the 1960s, it has similar features to Putney Leisure Centre – a 33m pool (which is why it tops my preferred list), L-shaped to include a deep diving area, with diving boards still intact. To that extent, it feels 'historic' in design and proportion.

There's a separate teaching pool, and a newer addition, dating from the 1980s, in the form of three flumes. These are the main attraction. Visitors have to pay extra to use the flumes, which are in a room set apart from the main pool area, although the 'landing area' – a small hot bubble pool – is within sight, just through some glass doors (which is handy to know if you're taking the opportunity to have a swim while your kids play).

The three flumes have different degrees of scariness: the Shark has a steep sudden drop; the Dolphin is gentler and longer; and you travel down the Whale on a huge rubber ring. It's seriously good fun for adults too. Within the pool there are designated times for 'inflatables', and their inflatable is no common or garden lilo. It's a massive, heavy, plastic, adventure structure lashed to the side of the pool; kids queue up repeatedly to take their turn to scramble through it, and off into the water at the other end. If you're here to swim while the inflatable is up, you'll be relegated to the diving area. Otherwise, you have one narrow lane. So during school holidays, it certainly is restricted.

Once they were all flumed out, and with the inflatables put away, my testers hit the pool. They played for over an hour, even though it was a

You're never too old to throw yourself down a water tunnel.

A sizeable pool for a peaceful swim, while everyone else is on the big flumes.

standard swimming pool – no beach, no 'fun time' activities. I imagined that something with MORE (slides, water poles, waves, volcanoes and earthquakes) would hit the top spot. But no – this was definitely it. This is a very busy pool generally – sub aqua, diving, tri and swimming clubs – so it's clearly a much-loved local facility too. Everything around it – the changing facilities and café – were fine, if unremarkable for waiting parents. Overall, it was a veritable hit.

White Oak Leisure Centre

Address Hilda May Avenue, Swanley, Kent BR8 7BT
Phone 01322 662 188
Web www.sencio.org.uk

HONOURABLE MENTIONS

If Guildford Spectrum was within the M25, it would go straight to the top of the list. Fighting it would be the Coral Reef in Bracknell, and Aquasplash in Hemel Hempstead. But if you're travelling outside London, make a detour to Pells Pool in Lewes, the oldest fresh-water public lido in the country. It's a beautiful place to swim or play, and there's enough lawn for picnicking.

Indoors again, if the refurbishment of Leyton Leisure Lagoon had been completed, I would certainly have tried it out (not least because it's always good to see pools being refurbished, even if their stated aim is not swimming). At the bottom of the charts languish Archway Leisure Centre (which has a flume and wave machines and hot tub) and Latchmere Leisure Centre (beachside, small slide and wave machine).

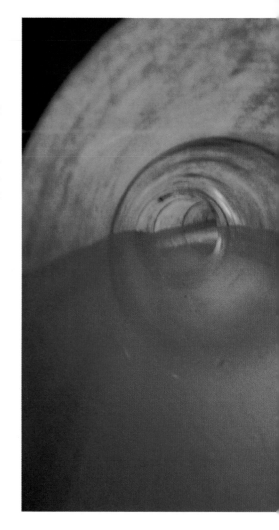